HEROES OF Cornwall

SHEILA BIRD

COUNTRYSIDE BOOKS
NEWBURY BERKSHIRE

First published 2004
© Sheila Bird 2004

All rights reserved. No reproduction permitted without the prior permission of the publisher:

COUNTRYSIDE BOOKS
3 Catherine Road
Newbury, Berks

To view our complete range of books, please visit us at www.countrysidebooks.co.uk

ISBN 1 85306 870 5

Designed by Peter Davies, Nautilus Design
Produced through MRM Associates Ltd., Reading
Printed by J.W. Arrowsmith Ltd., Bristol

CONTENTS

Dedication

To the crew of the Penlee Lifeboat *Solomon Browne*
who, in the grand, heroic tradition of the sea,
gave their lives while attempting to save others
on the night of 19th December 1981

Trevelyan Richards
Stephen Madron
Nigel Brockman
John Blewett
Charles Greenhaugh
Kevin Smith
Barrie Torrie
Gary Wallis

Foreword

Over the centuries the wild and windswept Cornish peninsula has produced countless heroes who endeavoured to glean a livelihood from the sea, the land and the mineral wealth which lay beneath the surface. Those who thrived in such a harsh environment were hardy and inventive, and this gave rise to some colourful characters with a homespun philosophy of their own.

In writing this book, I have interpreted the word 'hero' in a broad sense and it includes some rather eccentric folk heroes, who rose from obscurity to become part of the Cornish culture, and some classical heroes, who demonstrated outstanding courage and selflessness. Some of the stories may pull at the heartstrings, others may evoke a smile. They include up-to-date accounts of the valiant Penlee Lifeboat crew, and Hayle-born Rick Rescorla, hero of the Twin Towers.

Acknowledgements

My thanks to the staff of the Cornish Studies Library, The Cornwall Centre, Redruth for all their help, and acknowledgements to the following in regard to obtaining illustrations:

Bodmin Town Museum
Cornish Studies Library
Penlee Lifeboat Station
Royal Cornwall Museum, Truro
RNLI
Shire Hall, Bodmin
David Heathcote
Brian Stewart
H.G. Welby

1

John Couch Adams 1819–1892

Reaching for the Stars

Such bright examples of application and success, even under disadvantageous circumstances, ought to stimulate the young to exert their powers, and to prefer the honourable path of learning to the ignoble pursuits of dissipation and folly.

(John Allen: *History of Liskeard*, 1856)

It would be hard to find a more modest 'hero' than John Couch Adams. He was a native of Cornwall whose immense intellectual capacity enabled him to rise to great heights in the academic world, most especially in the field of astronomy. It was John Adams who discovered Neptune, although the actions of others and his self-effacing character meant that he very nearly did not receive the credit for this remarkable discovery.

John Couch Adams was the eldest of seven. He was born to Thomas and Tabitha Adams of Lidcott Farm, Laneast, on 5th January 1819, under the sign of Capricorn, the quietly determined goat.

The Adams family had been farming on the northern fringes of Bodmin Moor for generations. They were staunch Wesleyans and always took an active part in parish affairs. After his marriage to Tabitha Knill Grylls of Stoke Climsland, Thomas Adams and his bride took up the tenancy of Lidcott Farm, an isolated homestead owned by John King Lethbridge of nearby Tregeare.

Over the years the children helped out with the daily chores and although the eldest son, John, was not likely to follow in his father's footsteps, he enjoyed tending the sheep on Laneast

Lidcott Farm, Laneast, birthplace of John Couch Adams. (Royal Cornwall Museum)

Downs. He had a great affinity with nature and would sit and admire the commanding views across the wild and rolling moorland landscape. Most significantly, he liked to linger on after dusk, lying in the heather and gazing up at the stars with a deep sense of wonder. His father would chide his son for being out on the moors so late, and was unable to understand his eldest child's fascination with the skies. Perhaps he took after his mother's side of the family, who were more academic.

John's most cherished possession was a simple book on astronomy which had once belonged to his maternal grandfather. This gave him a basic understanding of the motions of the heavenly bodies, and he learned to distinguish the planets from the fixed stars.

Using this book as his guide, Adams would observe the rising and setting of the constellations. He identified Charles's Wain, revolving nightly about the most extreme star in what he called the tail of the Plough, and Orion with his twinkling belt and curved sword, 'writing on one knee', as he put it.

Having discovered his passion, Adams was single-minded in his pursuit of more knowledge. He carved a sundial which he placed on the window sill of the parlour, and created a cardboard sextant for taking the altitude of the sun. When he was first permitted to study the moon through a telescope he exclaimed, 'Why they have Brown Willy and Rough Tor up there!' (These were the two highest tors on Bodmin Moor.) It was a light-hearted, perceptive remark; likening the lunar landscape to the stark, weathered granitic landscape he knew so well.

John started his education at the local village school. His ability in mathematics and algebra, however, soon outstripped that of his schoolmaster. The enlightened teacher nurtured Adams's gift by plying him with books which would allow his young student to progress at his own pace.

One day John and his father visited a Mr G. Pearson of Sticklepath, near Okehampton, who had a son a little older than John. Whilst talking to the two boys Pearson was so struck with John's remarkable intellect that he took him to visit a neighbouring schoolmaster, who was astonished at his mathematical genius.

Mr Pearson went on to tell Mr Adams senior that his son would be a great man one day, adding, 'If he were my boy, I would sell the hat off my head, rather than not give him a good education.' As a result John was sent to a school in Devonport run by a relative of his mother. Even at this tender age, the boy was shy and modest amidst all the praise, an endearing characteristic which stayed with him all his life.

Adams came under the tutelage of Mr N. Foott of Rillaton, Linkinhorne, and Dr Martin of Lamerton, who prepared him for his university entrance. Throughout this time, Adams read astronomical works, obtained from the library of the Mechanics Institute, avidly; he drew maps of constellations and computed celestial phenomena. His aptitude for science had come to the notice of Mr J. J. Lethbridge, who with others helped him to take his place at Cambridge University at the age of twenty. At that time his account of a solar eclipse, as viewed through a small spyglass, was published in a London paper. After watching the night skies for three weeks, he was rewarded with the sight of Halley's Comet on 16th October 1839.

When he arrived in Cambridge in 1839, the cloistered confines of St John's College must have seemed like yet another planet to the young man born and raised on the open moors of Cornwall. But he had found his intellectual niche and took to it like a duck

John Couch Adams, from the painting by Thomas Mogford. (Royal Cornwall Museum)

to water. Adams entered the university as a sizar, which traditionally implied the payment of reduced fees and the duty of carrying out certain menial tasks. He took his degree aged 23 and then became Senior Wrangler, the student of highest merit in a mathematical tripos. It was not long before he was made a Fellow of St John's College.

Adams' greatest triumph, based on his philosophy of the reversed method of reasoning, from an unknown to a known, was his discovery of the planet Neptune in 1845, when he was just 26 years old. During the early 19th century many scientists had been baffled by the inexplicable behaviour of the planet Uranus, which failed to appear in its anticipated position in the sky at the appointed time. Adams, along with others, attributed the disturbance of Uranus to the pull of some as yet undiscovered planet. Here was an opportunity to put his hitherto untried mathematical means of working it out to the test. By the late summer of 1845 Adams had mapped out its probable track across the sky, and calculated the exact spot where the new planet could be observed with a powerful telescope.

The Astronomer Royal at the time was Sir George Airy, who was well known for his arrogance and his rather dismissive attitude towards the endeavours of others. He scorned those who were seeking to establish geology as a science, and was adept at shooting progressive thinkers down in flames. On one occasion when Sir William Hamilton was discussing some striking mathematical fact, Airy interjected, 'No, it cannot be so!' Somewhat taken aback Sir William explained that he had been investigating the subject closely for the last few months, and could not doubt its truth. 'But,' retorted Airy, 'I've been at it for the last five minutes, and cannot see it at all!'

When Adams submitted his mathematical evidence explaining the cause of the disturbances to Uranus, and his discovery of Neptune, the Astronomer Royal simply locked the papers away, perhaps indignant that a young upstart should presume to mark out such a revolutionary path in mathematical science. By doing this, Airy deprived Adams of staking his claim to being the first to discover the new planet; instead he had to share the honour with a young Frenchman.

When the French astronomer Urbain Le Verrier announced to the world that he had discovered the whereabouts of an unknown planet by means of a mathematical calculation, many English scientific feathers were ruffled. Neither Adams nor Le Verrier had known that they were both working on the same idea and a row rumbled on around Europe over who should get the credit.

The only one who appeared to be unconcerned about the confusion was young Adams himself. His modesty is recorded in a journal kept by Caroline Fox, who met the scientist at a dinner party in Carclew in 1847. She noted, 'He, in common with many others, conceived that there must be a planet to account for the disturbances of Uranus; and when he had the time he set to work at the process, in deep, quiet faith that the Fact was there, and that his hitherto untried mathematical path was the one which must reach it; that there were no anomalies in the Universe, but that even here, and now, they could be explained and included in a "Higher Law".' She went on to say that the delight of working it out was greater than any acknowledgement for his achievement; that his love of pure truth was an intense, inward necessity.

In the end Le Verrier sent his research to Johann Galle, an acquaintance of his at the Berlin Observatory, who sighted the planet on 24th September 1846, whereupon the French claimed the discovery. Airy later wrote to Le Verrier, mentioning the work which Adams had done and which had been sitting in his study. Adams, however, was unperturbed. When Prince Albert commiserated with him about this vexatious affair, the genial scientist replied, 'Oh! I hope we shall find another planet during your Royal Highness's Chancellorship!'

When the two 'rivals' eventually met at a British Association meeting in Oxford, it was with mutual respect and admiration, and the discovery of the planet Neptune came to be acknowledged as a joint achievement.

Adams was hailed as the greatest English astronomical scientist since Isaac Newton and was bestowed with various honours. He was awarded the Copley Medal by the Royal Society in 1848 and became a Fellow of the Society the following year. He was the President of the Royal Astronomical Society from 1851–53 and again from 1874–76. He also became Director of the Cambridge Observatory, and founded the Adams Prize. Not forgetting his roots, he was Vice President of the Royal Cornwall Polytechnic Society from 1875–7. Despite all these achievements he kept his feet firmly on the ground. In 1847 he declined the offer of a knighthood from Queen Victoria and in 1881 he turned down the opportunity to become Astronomer Royal.

In the late 1980s, when Voyager II was hurtling towards Neptune, the Lawrence House Museum in Launceston put on a Couch Adams exhibition. There was great excitement when it was reported that at 4 am on 25th August, Voyager, which had already discovered a third Neptune moon, would pass within 3,000 miles of the planet after a twelve-year flight. One astronomer declared, 'Only four people in history have ever discovered a planet, and one of them is a Cornishman.' The dispute rages on, and there was great indignation when, in April 2003, the Irish Astronomical Society in Dublin suggested that the Frenchman should receive full credit for the discovery of Neptune. Dark mutterings were heard in Cornwall of the Gallic penchant for rewriting history!

John Couch Adams died in Cambridge in January 1892 but there are several memorials to the celebrated Cornish astronomer, including plaques in Westminster Abbey and Truro Cathedral, as well as busts in Launceston and commemorative stones at Laneast.

2

Neville Northey Burnard (1818–1878)

From Obscurity to Fame . . .

The majestic church of St Nonna, traditionally known as 'the cathedral of the Moors', stands sentinel at the heart of the delightful moorland village of Altarnun, where a clear and sparkling stream glides swiftly beneath a handsome hump-backed granite bridge, as it has done for centuries. Anyone venturing up the narrow main street may notice a circular slate plaque on the wall of one of the cottages, recalling that this was the birthplace of the sculptor Neville Northey Burnard on 11th October 1818. His is a tale of a tortured Cornish genius, who went from rags to riches and back again.

Neville Northey Burnard's father was a stonemason, while his mother ran a little dame school, which young Neville attended until he started working full-time for his father at the age of ten. The Burnards were related to the Isbells of nearby Trewint, who had offered hospitality to the fiery preacher John Wesley, and were ardent disciples of the great man. The Wesleyan faith would have had a great influence on young Burnard in his formative years, but he was essentially a child of the moors and granite tors. He threw himself wholeheartedly into whatever he was doing and had a deep love of nature.

This son of hardy moorland stock grew into a fine strapping lad with broad shoulders and strong arms and a deft touch. He was as capable of carrying heavy materials around as he was of performing the most intricate of tasks with his hands. Learning the art of stonemasonry from his father, Burnard soon became fascinated by the traditionally ornate craftsmanship which could be seen in many of the local churches. He was particularly struck

NEVILLE NORTHEY BURNARD (1818–1878)

Self portrait of Burnard, aged 56. (Royal Cornwall Museum)

with the sensitively sculptured slate tomb effigies, like those at North Hill, later described by Nikolaus Pevsner as 'the most endearing monuments in Cornwall'. Acting as mortar boy to his father, handling slate, granite, bricks and plaster, he established an affinity with these materials, which were to form the basis of his creativity.

From the very start Burnard was a natural artist, with a sense of design. He made sketches on wood, slate or anything else he could find, using improvised tools. He would sketch angels, experimenting with shapes and creating heads and other forms out of stone or wood. He found that slate, sometimes referred to as 'Cornish marble', offered the ideal medium. His designs were heavily influenced by his surroundings, drawing on the shapes of the local flora and fauna as well as the traditional motifs that had captured his imagination in Cornish churches and fine houses. The spirit of the Cornish countryside and the rural way of life were all reflected in the young Burnard's self-taught early efforts.

When he was just twelve years old, a family tragedy gave Burnard the opportunity to apply his skills. He cut a small headstone for his nine year old cousin's grave in the churchyard at Altarnun, carving the letters into relief with long sharpened nails. Two years later he prepared a tombstone for his grandparents, inscribed, 'Sacred to the memory of George and Elizabeth Burnard'. He created a relief of an angel in flight against the sun's rays at the head of the inscription, with embellishments of delicate weeping willow fronds. The stone featured regularly patterned raised first words.

During his teens, Burnard was offered a great opportunity. When the Cornish industrialist Joseph Thomas Treffry acquired prestigious Place House in Fowey, with its battlemented walls, towers and highly ornate bays, the discerning tradesman John Whale of Altarnun took a major part in selecting a team of specialist craftsmen able to renovate and extend the historical property in sympathetic style. It was a team which included the promising 15 year old Burnard, who took full advantage of this invaluable experience. He was employed to carry stone, and model numerous medallions and other lavish embellishments in plaster, reminiscent of the style displayed on the walls of Launceston church. He must have been struck by the use of the finest polished specimens of porphyry, jasper and porphyritic granite in the entrance hall, and the merging of Georgian and Gothic characteristics. The ambitious young man was noticed by the dynamic Treffry who took an interest in his sketches and creativity, and allowed him to make use of his library.

It was actually a very mundane purchase which was to change Burnard's life. In 1835 he bought a copy of *The Penny Magazine* and was captivated by the grace and beauty of the human form, as depicted in the woodcut of the Laocoon statue on the cover. He used it as the basis for a bas relief in Delabole slate, which he submitted to the Royal Cornwall Polytechnic Society in Falmouth. They were amazed that an untaught lad of 16 'from an obscure village' could have created such a work of art with homemade tools and he was awarded a Silver Medal for his efforts.

His next commission was much closer to home and can still be seen today. In 1795, the Methodist Society had transferred its meeting place from the Isbells' cottage at Trewint to the chapel next door to Burnard's home. Some years later it was in need of enlarging and in 1836 the 18 year old Burnard created a delightful portrait sculpture of John Wesley above the chapel door. He chose to create the sculpture using locally quarried Polyphant stone, containing silicates of magnesium and iron, producing a rather sombre greyish blue effect, with flecks of brown and red.

Following his success with the Royal Cornwall Polytechnic Society, new opportunities opened up for him. The Society's first president, Sir Charles Lemon, encouraged him to try his luck in London and introduced him to Sir Francis Chantry, the leading sculptor of the day.

The young Burnard was totally at home in the capital and mixed easily with fashionable society. He met many notable people from the world of art who influenced and guided him. Amongst them were the notable sculptors Baily, Marshall and Foley, and also the artist G. F. Watts, with whom he formed a friendship. They encouraged him to be more disciplined, practical and

Burnard's birthplace in Altarnun (centre). His sculpture of the evangelist John Wesley can be seen above the door of the old chapel on the left of the picture. (Royal Cornwall Museum)

businesslike in regard to earning his living as a sculptor. Surrounded by such stimulating people Burnard threw himself enthusiastically into the social, creative and cultural London scene, studying hard and emulating the works of old masters and leading contemporaries, as well as experimenting with new techniques. He was an engaging young man and society took this gifted, fine figure of a Cornishman to their hearts. His reputation as a sculptor grew and the commissions rolled in.

It was Burnard's outstanding talent, and possibly his Cornish background, that earned him a commission by Royal Appointment. He was asked to sculpt a bust of Queen Victoria's six year old son, who, as well as being Prince of Wales, was also Duke of Cornwall, and destined to become Edward VII.

NEVILLE NORTHEY BURNARD (1818–1878)

Burnard exhibited at the Royal Academy in 1855, 1858, 1866 and 1867, and made immortal the features of many personalities in the world of science, art, literature, astronomy, religion and politics, including Gladstone, Thackeray, General Lord Gough, G.B. Greenhough, the first president of the Geological Society, Professor Edward Forbes FRC, and Harriet Beecher Stowe (author of *Uncle Tom's Cabin*), which was financed by the anti-slavery movement in England. When Ebenezer Elliott, the 'corn law rhymer' and hymn writer associated with the Chartist movement, died in 1849, Burnard was chosen to create a statue of him to be erected in Sheffield. He also made a marble bust of Beethoven for the Musical Union in London.

He carried out commissions for many notable Cornish personalities, including Charles Buller, MP for Liskeard and one-time president of the Poor Law Board; Sir Charles Lemon; Lord Falmouth; and Joseph Thomas Treffry.

He was proud to have been born 'less than an hour's walk from the birthplace of the celebrated astronomer' John Couch Adams, and was delighted when he was successful in obtaining a commission to execute a bust of the great man in 1848. It received a Silver Medal at the Polytechnic Exhibition that year. Both men were guests of the cultured Fox family of Penjerrick and Falmouth, who did much to encourage the rising young stars of the scientific and artistic world.

Burnard revelled in the glamorous life which went with the accolades but never forgot his home. He made frequent visits to Cornwall and carried out many fine commissions. He would entertain Cornish society with tales of the London scene. On one occasion he spoke of sculptors who sometimes felt out of their depth in trying to keep abreast of conversations with intellectual sitters, and recalled the case of his master, Sir Francis Chantry, who, having reached his limit with Lord Melbourne, saved the situation by requesting, 'Would your Lordship kindly turn your head on the other side and shut your mouth!'

While at the height of his fame in London he met and married Mary Ann Nicholson, a talented artist herself. They lived in a house in Pimlico and had two sons and two daughters. One son, Thomas Burnard, was to later exhibit at the Royal Academy between 1868 and 1886.

After a charmed existence of 30 years or more, Burnard started to show signs of restlessness and sink into depression. It was as if the dynamic driving force which had carried him from success to success had turned in on him and he developed an antipathy towards conventional society. He turned his back on both his wife and his work and sought consolation in alcohol. Old friends would shy away from him and, as all his motivation ebbed away, so the numbers of commissions fell, leading to the closure of his studio.

Mary Ann had an artistic brother, who had been attracted by the unique quality of the landscape and the famous stone on the wild and windswept Isle of Portland. When he fell ill in the spring of 1870, she hurried off to Dorset to nurse him, taking the two younger children with her. Unfortunately they both contracted scarlet fever soon after their arrival and sadly the couple's youngest, 11 year old Lottie, died on 7th March. It was to be a double tragedy, for her uncle died the following day.

This was a bitter blow for Burnard. Lottie had been his favourite and he was devastated. The extent of his feelings was revealed in the poignant, delicately carved headstone in the churchyard of St Nicholas in Broadway, just outside Weymouth, depicting them both in profile, with the symbolism of the artist's palette and a broken lily.

Following on from this traumatic experience, Burnard packed his things and returned to East Cornwall, where he found temporary respite in the homes of childhood friends. His spirit was broken and he was probably suffering from a nervous breakdown. Nevertheless, he tried to eke out a living by writing political satire and poetry for local newspapers and making sketches of local personalities, periodically lapsing into drunkenness and despair, and wandering the lanes like a vagrant.

One dark and howling night towards the end of 1875, the Dawe family of Crow's Nest near St Cleer were surprised to hear a knock at the door and behold a dishevelled figure of titanic build, who pleaded for a night's shelter in gentlemanly tones. It turned out to be Burnard, who, having been served with refreshment, bounced back into one of his entertaining moods, yarning away for the rest of the night. He remained with the family and managed not to touch a drop of alcohol. He produced light-hearted poems in dialect and some fine sketches depicting the Cheesewring, Trevethy Quoit and other features of the granite landscape, as well as one of the Cornish metaphysician Samuel Drew, which he presented to the Dawes.

Three years later he was back on the bottle and back on the road. He called at the White Hart Hotel in Camborne, where he was taken ill with a heart and kidney complaint. The wayward genius and former darling of the London scene was sent to the workhouse in Redruth, where he died on 27th November 1878. The man who had so compassionately honoured others in death with his artistry was buried in an unmarked pauper's grave in the churchyard at Camborne. Ironically one of his finest marble sculptures 'Sacred to the memory of the Rev Hugh Rogers, BA' is inside on the north wall of this parish church. A medallion marble of Dr George Smith similarly graced the nearby Wesleyan Chapel in Camborne.

Camborne Old Cornwall Society erected a simply inscribed Delabole slate tombstone 76 years later, and it was the Cornish poet Charles Causley who was instrumental in having the plaque placed on Burnard's birthplace in 1968.

Although his story had an unhappy and lonely ending the legacy of Neville Northey Burnard lives on in many churches and churchyards, museums, stately homes and statues in Cornwall.

3

Mary Bryant (nee Broad) born 1765

A Remarkable Tale of Survival

The heroine in this chapter has more of the fictitious Moll Flanders about her than the characteristics of a Florence Nightingale or some other worthy female role model. Mary Broad was a wild child, who found herself transported to Australia, alongside other convicts who had managed to avoid the death penalty for their misdemeanours. Through sheer determination and willpower, and after many adventures, Mary eventually returned to England. She was saved from prison by a generous and well-known benefactor and given a comfortable living in London before returning to the town of her birth, Fowey, to live out the rest of her days in relative obscurity.

Like Defoe's eponymous heroine, Mary used her wits. A strong character with a great deal of intelligence, she also learned to use her charms as a woman when it suited her and took advantage of anyone willing to offer her a helping hand. She managed to pack into a few years far more adventures than many of us would see in a lifetime but, even after all her wild escapades, she was still welcomed back by her family.

It was around 1760 that William Broad, a young Fowey mariner and fisherman, returned from sea and married his sweetheart Grace. In January 1763 their firstborn child, also called Grace, was christened. She was a gentle, sweet-natured girl, and came to be known affectionately as Dolly. Grace gave birth to their second daughter, Mary, two years later, who was demanding, skinny, hyperactive, and quite unlike her sister. Sadly, another daughter died at birth, and they lost their only son at the age of six months. The surviving sisters grew up strong and healthy, and became particularly close to their older cousin Elizabeth Broad. In later years, Elizabeth along with her husband Edward Puckey was to be instrumental in persuading Mary to return to Fowey.

Mary was always a tomboy and was accepted as 'one of the lads'. She was a skilled mariner but also a charming and practised flirt, all of which stood her in good stead when it came to her fight for survival. Traditionally the mariners' life was a man's life. Women might turn out to assist with the launching of the lifeboat, or help with the fish trade on the quayside, but generally they were expected to stay at home, look after the children and have a meal on the table when their menfolk returned home from the sea. Not only that, but there was a deep-rooted superstition about women in boats bringing bad luck.

The late 18th century was a time of hardship and social unrest and in order to bring some kind of order, the ruling classes were quick to hand out harsh punishments. Since the American War of Independence, it was no longer possible to transport convicts to the Americas; therefore prisons were full to overflowing and the authorities were finding it increasingly difficult to cope with the number of inmates.

One such offender was a fisherman named William Bryant, whose fate was to be closely allied to that of Mary. He was brought to trial at the Launceston Assizes for 'feloniously and knowingly receiving contraband cargo and using the name of Timothy Cary'. He was acquitted on the first indictment, but found guilty of forgery, on account of having attempted to pass himself off as Timothy Cary. He was sentenced to seven years' transportation and confined in a Cornish gaol in the meantime. Long drawn out sentences like this were intended as a deterrent to others.

In 1785, the people of Fowey experienced a particularly difficult year. The fishing failed and the poor were at risk of starvation. By this time Dolly had gone into service, but her rebellious 19 year old sister had taken to living rough in the wooded area of the Tamar Valley and committing highway robbery. Her life of crime was brought to an abrupt close in January 1786, when she and two female accomplices set upon one Agnes Lakeman on the road to Plymouth. When the victim tried to resist, Mary attacked and beat her before seizing her silken bonnet and other personal items to the value of eleven guineas. After being captured, the three culprits were taken before a local magistrate, and then cast into gaol to await the Exeter Lenten Assizes.

Confinement in a dark, cold cell, and a possible death sentence hanging over her, must have come as a shock to the free-spirited Mary. In March, she, along with a group of others, was transported over Dartmoor in an open cart, their legs shackled with irons. She was condemned to death at Exeter and taken to gaol. Four days later, she was told that her sentence had been

Some convicts remained in leg irons aboard the prison hulks when in port, or as punishment for bad behaviour.
(Photograph by the author, courtesy of Bodmin Town Museum)

commuted to seven years' transportation, an order signed by the Right Honourable Thomas, Lord Sydney, a Principal Secretary of State.

The prisoners found themselves being carted off to Devonport and put aboard the prison hulk *Dunkirk*, one of the obsolete warships being used to contain some of the many convicts awaiting transportation. The unwieldy, weather-beaten hulk, at anchor in the busy Hamoase, had been dismasted and adapted for her unaccustomed penal role, with all portholes and hatches on the landward side firmly secured. Mary found herself under the guard of a detachment of marines, including Cornishman Watkin Tench, who had a more humanitarian approach than most.

As each wretched creature shuffled aboard, names, physical characteristics and details of the crimes were documented before they were cast into the dark and stinking bowels of the vessel. It was not a pleasant experience below deck, with so many bodies crammed into such a confined area and only a strong curtain of metal railings segregating the sexes. William Bryant was one of those held in the same ship.

After a prolonged period of indecision in regard to where this undesirable section of society might be deposited, fear of an imminent epidemic prompted the authorities to set their sights on establishing a penal colony on the shores of Botany Bay in New South Wales, which associates of the late Captain Cook had considered suitable for this purpose. Plans were made to provide sufficient vessels, provisions and equipment to transport hundreds of convicts to Australia and sustain them for the first two years. Captain Arthur Phillip was to be the first Governor of the new colony and was to sail aboard the warship *Sirius*.

During the preparation for this epic journey, some of the male prisoners were taken ashore in labouring gangs, while the women were left in the hulk of the *Dunkirk*. The more astute used their feminine charms to offer favours to their custodians in return for certain privileges. In true Moll Flanders style, Mary fell pregnant during this time, although she never revealed the name of the father of the child she was to bear at sea.

The six transports commissioned for the First Fleet were fitted out at Deptford, before being placed off Woolwich, Portsmouth and Plymouth. They were to be escorted by three supply ships and two warships, with some of the officers and marines taking their families.

On 7th January 1787, Mary was one of those taken from the *Dunkirk* to stay overnight below Plymouth's Citadel, before being rowed out to the waiting transport, the *Charlotte*. William Bryant was also put on this ship, along with a range of other petty thieves and hardened criminals, while others they had got to know went aboard the *Friendship*.

After 10 months on the *Dunkirk*, the pregnant Mary had to endure even worse conditions on the *Charlotte*. There was scarcely any light in this vastly overcrowded, claustrophobic environment, and little prospect of illicit visits to officers' cabins up on deck. They had been told that they would be allowed on deck as soon as they left home waters to rendezvous with the rest of the fleet at the Motherbank off Portsmouth, but as it happened their departure was delayed by storms and foggy conditions, which meant that the inmates of both transports were confined below decks for almost a fortnight.

By the time the fleet set sail for Botany Bay on Sunday, 13th May, 1787, Mary had reached the age of 22. The convicts remained below deck as they headed briskly down the Channel to rendezvous off the Isles of Scilly, with sails a-billowing, passing so near, yet so far, from the port of Fowey, and Mary's relatives. When she vowed to return to Cornwall one day, there were very few who thought she would ever achieve her goal.

Life became a little more bearable once they reached the open sea, with regular periods on deck and the opportunity to remain free of the irons and shackles if they behaved themselves. Mary was bright enough to realise that she had to make a good impression and stay on the right side of authority in order to make her life easier. The more relaxed regime enabled her to make new friends and renew her acquaintance with William Bryant and Watkin Tench among others.

Whenever the ship put into a port, the prisoners had to remain below deck. They envied the officers and men, who could go ashore freely while new provisions and fresh water were brought on board. Conditions below became close to unbearable, with cockroaches and rats swarming around and the stench of rotting debris filling the air.

Mary gave birth to a daughter in the South Atlantic on 3rd September, four days out of Rio. The little girl was christened Charlotte in Cape Town on 28th October by the Reverend Richard Johnson. As they got closer to their destination, the convicts were encouraged to regularise any illicit liaisons by getting married upon disembarkation.

William Bryant and Mary Broad were amongst those who gave their names to the Reverend Johnson. This was no love match made in Heaven, but both could see the practical advantages of joining forces. As far as William was concerned it was a good idea to have a woman of his own, as they were in short supply, although he never regarded the marriage as legally binding. Mary for her part could see William was a strong and capable man who could protect her and Charlotte. Both harboured ambitions of making an escape.

On 19th January 1788 they got their first sight of mainland Australia. The 15,000 mile voyage had taken the fleet eight months, with the loss of 48 lives, 40 of whom were convicts.

Botany Bay in high summer seemed remarkably hot and brown and inhospitable, and not the promising rich and fertile environment the new arrivals had expected. Captain Phillip went ashore with some of the crew to pacify the natives with trinkets and beads. In the end the fleet sailed northwards into Port

Jackson, one of the finest natural harbours in the world. It was decided to name the cove where the penal settlement was to be established in honour of Lord Sydney. The majestic, capacious harbour was a far cry from the centuries old port of Fowey, where Mary's ancestors had been seafarers. Captain Phillip also sent a detachment of marines and convicts to claim Norfolk Island to the east, before the French ships, which had been sighted in Botany Bay, arrived.

The harsh reality of starting up a new life now set in. Supplies were running low, and the practical skills of the convicts were to play a large part in the setting up of the colony. William Bryant assisted the troops in clearing the bush and erecting a tented encampment before the other convicts came ashore. He had won the trust of the guards and officers during the latter stages of the voyage and was a trusted go-between. Aside from his practical skills, William was also an experienced fisherman, who could prove vital to their survival.

William used his new-found position to his advantage. He insisted on a separate hut for himself and his family. He retained a percentage of the fish caught and enjoyed other privileges. Mary was happy to benefit from this, while strengthening her resolve to return with her family to Cornwall.

William was allowed to use the Governor's boat for his fishing expeditions and Mary and their old friend Watkin Tench helped him with the nets and lines. The Bryants also made allies of the native Aborigines, thereby creating enemies amongst fellow convicts who did not enjoy the same freedom.

The colonists owed much to the efforts of the Reverend Johnson and a former Cornish farm labourer called James Rose, who had almost completed his sentence, and who ultimately made a great success of life in Australia with his convict wife. The assumption that this penal colony would soon become self-sufficient, however, was a false one, for it was short of experienced farmers and the machinery needed to cultivate the virgin land. It also lacked skilled carpenters needed for the construction of basic facilities and to build boats to extend the fishing activities. Illness caused by malnutrition was rife, and food shortages led to dire warnings to anyone who was tempted to steal provisions. There was also an acute shortage of medical supplies.

These food shortages led to William's right to a percentage of the fishing catch being withdrawn. He defied this edict but was betrayed by Joseph Paget, a fellow convict who had been with them on the *Dunkirk* and the *Charlotte*. William received 100 lashes, lost his fishing responsibilities and his marital home. With mounting unrest threatening to destroy the future of the whole colony, punishments got harsher. The Governor dispatched a crew on the *Sirius* to Cape Town for more provisions and sent another group of convicts to Norfolk Island.

William regained his role in the fisheries and his family returned to their home, but the couple's plans for escape were put on hold for a while when Mary fell pregnant again. But, by using the Governor's boat for fishing three nights a week, William was able to put preparations into place without arousing suspicion.

Mary and William's son, Emanuel, was born on 4th April 1790. The following day came the unwelcome news of a shipwreck, scuppering Port Jackson's chances of receiving supplies in the foreseeable future. Rations were cut back further and some convicts became too weak to work. When the Second Fleet of convicts arrived soon afterwards they found a demoralised camp, low on supplies, rather than the thriving colony they were expecting. Many of the prisoners on the Second Fleet had spent the whole voyage below deck chained up, which meant more sick and weak individuals adding to the already ailing community. Furthermore, a Third Fleet was on its way.

Although William had almost served his time, men with family responsibilities were not permitted to leave the country. So he and Mary had hatched a plan to escape to the Dutch East Indies in the Governor's boat, using navigational knowledge gleaned from the Aborigines. Then they unexpectedly found another ally. Captain Detmer Smith, of the Dutch vessel *Waaksamheyd*, had arrived at the colony, and, whilst he did not endear himself to those in authority, he became great friends with the Bryants.

Mary offered him her own style of hospitality. They found they were able to take the Captain into their confidence, and he supplied them with navigational instruments, muskets and ammunition, as well as water containers and food, which they concealed under their floorboards. Having enlisted seven trusted men to join them on their daring adventure, they planned to escape towards the end of February, before the monsoon season.

Their plans were delayed when the boat was damaged after capsizing and William nearly drowned. This turned out to be a blessing in disguise, for during repairs William was able to make sure the boat was even sturdier than it had been previously and better able to cope with the long voyage ahead.

The departure of Captain Smith and the *Waaksamheyd* served as a distraction from the quiet slipping away of the Bryant family and their 'crew', ably assisted by an Aborigine friend. One can only guess at the surprise and embarrassment on the morning of 29th March 1791 when it was discovered that the boat had gone, with its motley crew making good their escape.

With her strength of character, Mary was instrumental in sustaining the morale of her fellow escapees during the difficult journey ahead. The plan was to make for East Timor, and they made brief excursions ashore along the way to gather in fresh food and water and check the boat over. The delay in their departure meant they experienced some very violent storms but Mary did not lose heart. When the exhausted men were ready to give up, prepared to meet their destiny, Mary rallied them round and told them to keep on bailing while she put all her strength into controlling the tiller. After the storm came the calm, fraught with yet more danger. First they had to navigate the rocky reefs, before passing through the Torres Strait, into the Arafura Sea.

Somehow they survived all of this and arrived at Timor on 5th June 1791, after a remarkable voyage lasting 69 days and covering 3,254 miles. This was the stuff of fiction. The combination of William's seamanship and Mary's determination to succeed against all odds had got them through. Moll Flanders herself could not have fared any better on such an adventure and this voyage alone was enough to rival any author's imagination.

On their arrival at Kupang, William passed himself off as William Broad, and claimed to be the mate of a vessel wrecked off the Great Barrier Reef. He even said that other survivors might well turn up in more boats. The Dutch Governor was happy to attend to their needs and they soon found employment and adjusted to their new found freedom. Unfortunately, William returned to heavy drinking and started muttering about leaving his family and taking off for England on his own.

Little did the Bryants know that their cover was soon to be blown. The HMS *Pandora* had been despatched to track down the mutineers from HMS *Bounty*, who had famously overthrown their leader, Captain Bligh. After capturing some of them on Tahiti the *Pandora* was wrecked off the coast of Queensland. When four open boats with survivors arrived at Kupang, just 102 days after the convicts' arrival, they were surprised to be told that some of their 'shipmates' had already been there for several weeks. In the event, the convicts were taken aboard the *Kembang*, chained by the ankles as before and confined below deck. They were taken to Batavia where the sick were sent to the hospital and the others put aboard a ship of the Dutch East India Company. Sadly, little Emanuel died in the hospital on 1st December, where his now dispirited father also lost his fight for life shortly afterwards. Mary now had sole responsibility for Charlotte but remained determined to return home.

The convicts were moved from ship to ship, and both Mary and Charlotte were infected with fever. In 1792 they were put aboard

HMS *Gorgon* in Table Bay, en route from Port Jackson to England, where unbelievably Mary met up with her old friend Watkin Tench who was now a captain. With friends in the right places, Mary received more humane treatment on the voyage home but sadly Charlotte did not pull through, and the little girl, who was born at sea, died and was buried at sea.

The next chapter in Mary's life was to begin. She was alone and had lost all that was dear to her but she was not to be beaten.

Towards the end of June 1792 Mary set foot on English soil again, for the first time in five and a half years. And what a rollercoaster time it had been. She was packed off to Newgate Prison, and her plight, along with that of her fellow surviving prisoners, was reported in the *London Chronicle* with a potted version of their exploits. The *Dublin Chronicle*, however, printed a much more colourful and romantic version of events, worthy of Daniel Defoe himself, which captured the imagination of the public and turned the little band into folk heroes.

When the famous literary figure James Boswell, a lawyer (and some might add lecher), heard the story, he hastened to Newgate Prison to meet the dark haired young Cornish woman with the arresting big grey eyes, to see how he could help her. No doubt Mary was quick to use her feminine wiles to charm the old rogue. When she stood up in court Mary spoke clearly and intelligently and was sorry for the original offence she had committed all those years ago. Like a hero going into battle she told how she had risked everyone's lives in an open boat on treacherous seas because 'it was better to die than return to Botany Bay'. This really stuck a chord with the public and won her a great deal of sympathy. The press pleaded a case for mercy towards a woman who had surely repaid her debt to society, and the smitten Boswell pulled influential strings with renewed vigour. Meanwhile, well-wishers produced the wherewithal to make Mary's life in prison as comfortable as possible. She surely must have been a charming and charismatic woman.

On 2nd May 1793, Mary received her free pardon 'By His Majesty's Command', signed by the then Home Secretary, Henry Dundas. Boswell set her up in lodgings in Little Titchfield Street and provided Mary with pretty clothes and a comfortable lifestyle. The news that the portly old boy with his 'reputation' had secured a free pardon for the famous 'girl from Botany Bay' gave rise to mirth and ribald remarks in some quarters.

Later on that year, a Fowey man called on Boswell and asked for news of Mary, on behalf of the Broad family. He said that her father had come into a lot of money, and that Dolly, who was in service in London, would like to see her. The prodigal daughter was very sceptical about this but any doubts were banished when she enjoyed a tearful reunion with her virtuous and pretty sister, Dolly.

This was followed up by letters from Mary's cousin Elizabeth, with whom she had grown up, and her husband Ned Puckey. They wrote to Boswell imploring him to persuade Mary to return to her family in Fowey. Mary was comfortable in London, but Boswell thought it was her duty to return, even though he was reluctant to see her go, and fixed her up with an annuity of £10.

Mary returned home as she had left, by sea. She boarded the *Anne and Elizabeth* on 13th October and returned to the bosom of her family a free woman, ready to face whatever adventures the future might hold for her after her heroic struggle for liberty.

4

Billy Bray (1794–1868)

The Cornish Miner-Preacher

Billy Bray was essentially a man of his time and of his social and industrial environment, which allowed him scope to plough his distinctive furrow in a colourful and eccentric way. He went from being a debauched and wild young miner, with a work hard, play hard mentality, to being one of the most charismatic and fervent preachers of his day.

When the evangelist John Wesley and his followers had ventured into Cornwall for the first time, on 29th August 1743, long before Billy was born, it felt like entering a foreign land. The locals, who spoke in a strange tongue, had never seen a religious leader who rode around on horseback, preaching wherever he fancied, without seeking the authority of the vicar of the parish. The preacher and his followers were treated with suspicion and a certain amount of hostility. Wesley did, however, strike a chord with the miners of Redruth, where he preached on many occasions in the natural amphitheatre of Gwennap Pit.

Wesley brought a message of hope to the impoverished miners. He offered a distraction from the drudgery of their lives, toiling underground, living from hand to mouth in squalid hovels, with their only refuge the local ale house. Among those influenced by the teachings of Wesley were the Bray family of Twelveheads. They took to singing hymns, reading Bible texts, smartening up their humble homes and tending their neglected vegetable patches.

Grandfather Bray had been one of Wesley's most ardent followers and his son, who had enjoyed the benefits it had brought to family life, followed dutifully in his father's footsteps.

BILLY BRAY (1794–1868)

His grandson was another matter. Born on 1st June 1794 and baptised William Trewartha Bray at Gwennap church, he turned out to be a rebel and looked set to become the black sheep of the family.

Young Billy, who had several brothers and sisters, was a born show-off, who liked to be the life and soul of the party. His early upbringing was too devout for such an extrovert and he hated the discipline of chapel, with its boring preachers and emphasis on sin and damnation. Rebellion was more his style than religion, although he did benefit from the Methodist culture with its hymns and texts, which meant he knew how to read at a time when education was a privilege enjoyed by few.

Billy joined his father working at the tin mine at an early age, as was the custom. But when his father died he went to live with his grandfather at Twelveheads. This was an uneasy experience for all concerned, not just because of the huge generation gap. The teenage rebel labelled the Methodists 'a bunch of old hypocrites', and would mock and mimic the chapel-goers. When he was with his fellow miners he would always make jokes and remarks which were more bawdy and salacious than the rest. He was frustrated at his grandfather's strict regime. It was the last straw when he was forbidden to join his mates for a few drinks at the kiddleywink (beer shop), and so young Billy took himself off to mine in Devonshire.

Once he had escaped from his family, Billy went completely wild. He chose his own company, spent his own money and went drinking and whoring to his heart's content. Most of the time he was witty and amusing to be with, but when he got drunk he became aggressive and violent. When it came to foolish escapades during those Devon days, Billy was always at the forefront. Once he and his drunken cronies leapt on the back of a carthorse and were lucky to escape with their lives when the poor beast stumbled in the dark and sent them flying in all directions.

On another occasion a brawl turned into a pitched battle, during which his miner's helmet fell into the fire. He narrowly escaped gaol after stealing a replacement from another miner. He was to put these misdemeanours to good use in later life, holding his own past up as a bad example and a warning to others not to stray.

The event which was to shake Billy most of all was when he heard the ominous sound of rumbling while he was at work in the mine. He escaped moments before tons of rock fell where he had just been standing, and there were critical mutterings among some about the devil looking after his own. Although Billy made a point of not going to chapel, he found he had an uneasy conscience after this brush with death and a growing conflict arose within him. He became torn apart by fear and contrition and had a sneaking desire to reform.

After reading John Bunyan's *Visions of Heaven and Hell*, he felt he could never attain the former, and was gripped with terrifying visions of the latter. Billy dreaded falling asleep for fear of waking up in hell, and, although he had travelled to Devon seven years earlier to escape the rigid demands of chapel folk, he decided it was time to return across the Tamar in the hope of releasing himself from the devil's clutches.

It was another five years before Billy was to find complete peace of mind, mainly because he kept his inner conflict to himself. Billy feared being lampooned in the way he had so mercilessly lampooned others. If his family had been pleased to welcome their errant kinsman back to the fold, their joy soon turned to dismay when he began telling tales of his debauchery in Devon and staggered around in a drunken state. Even some of his cronies were shocked by his swearing and cursing, and recoiled from him in horror. Some were wont to say, 'Poor ole Billy 'as the look of the devil 'isself!'

Three years after his return, Billy married a miner's daughter called Joey. She was also a lapsed Methodist, and the service was conducted at Kea church in 1821 by Richard Polwhele, the famous writer and historian and also a critic of Methodism.

The young woman must have known that life with Billy would not be a bed of roses, yet he had charm and was fun to be with when he was sober, when his rather nondescript face would become radiant with merriment. Joey was also to experience the humiliation and hardship that came with being married to a drunkard, particularly when the money needed to feed and clothe the growing family was wasted in the ale house. On one occasion when Billy set out to fetch some coal for the fire, he called at the beer shop, which resulted in Joey going out to find him, and wheeling the heavy load home herself.

Billy was drinking himself sick. His conscience was tormenting him by day and his nightmares, filled with Dantesque imagery, left him rolling around in terror by night. His best friend Sam Coad did his best to cheer him up, while his wife, who had herself fallen by the wayside, urged him to 'seek the Lord'. This proved to be a turning point for the troubled man. After several days of reading aloud from the Bible, singing Wesleyan hymns, shouting prayers and chanting positive words and phrases, Billy finally felt he had been released from his burden of fear and guilt.

His shouts of joy left his workmates bemused. 'They said I was a *mad* man, but they meant I was a *glad* man!' declared the reformed Billy. 'And, glory be to God, I've been glad ever since!'

The world now seemed a brighter and fresher place to Billy. If John Bunyan's vision of hell had filled him with horror, the writer's vision of heaven was an inspiration which he wanted to share with others in his uniquely colourful and extrovert way.

Initially it was not plain sailing. As he had once feared, some of his old mates who used to laugh *with* him were now laughing *at* him. Some were embarrassed or angered by his pushiness when it came to preaching as they toiled down the mine, while others, who had realised the depths of his despair, were moved to tears by his transformation and were keen to follow his lead.

At that time the Wesleyan-inspired revival had broken into a number of splinter groups and Billy favoured the Bible Christians. On his first attempt to return to the fold he walked for miles along a rough and muddy track to a chapel in the pouring rain. But nobody else turned up. There was great rejoicing at Hicks Mill chapel the following Sunday, however, when he responded to the call of the class leader by telling his story in a lively and compelling way. Billy was in his element and felt as if he were walking on air as he made his way home to tell Joey of 'a joy unspeakable, and full of glory'.

It soon became evident that Billy had star quality, which kept folk on their toes and filled chapels. Indeed, if Billy were alive today, then, like his American namesake Billy Graham, he would surely be at home filling vast arenas or on one of the many religious channels preaching and chanting to the mass of adoring followers.

He became affectionately known as 'Little Billy Bray' and was soon accepted as a lay preacher on the local circuit. This remarkable man of humble origin remained the most colourful personality to preach from Cornish pulpits for over 40 years. He sang and danced for joy at every opportunity, styling himself 'the King's Son'. This wiry little chap with bushy eyebrows and a vibrant personality must have travelled thousands of miles on foot or on horseback to venues all over the county, where he preached in exuberant style, wearing a neat black suit and white bow tie. His enduring fame was destined to spread throughout Cornwall and far beyond.

Although Billy's chapel activities sometimes cut across his work as a miner, he had an understanding mine captain who adapted his tasks and accommodated his needs. The budding evangelist drew on everyday mining experiences, to which his listeners could relate, to illustrate points in his sermon. He always spoke in the third person (like a certain volatile trade union leader of modern times), which conveyed a sense of superiority and gave more impetus to his delivery.

The self-styled 'King's Son', who made an enduring contribution to Cornish culture. (Sheila Bird collection)

Any temptations, doubts or setbacks he may have experienced were attributed to the devil, and these were dispelled by giving 'Old Smutty Face' a stern and contemptuous talking-to and sending him packing with his forked tail between his legs. He turned negative situations into positive ones by recounting imaginary conversations with the tempter, turning the tables and shooting the wicked old fellow down in flames.

Services in the chapels would always begin in fairly traditional style, with a sermon, Bible readings and hymns, but then things would become more exciting as Billy warmed to his theme. He would challenge and prick the consciences of some of the congregation, crying 'Glory Hallelujah!' and 'Jesus forever!', before dancing a jig or two. Deep solemnity could be followed a moment later by raucous hilarity. And it didn't stop there. After the meeting things became even more noisy and hectic when groups of people were testifying and pouring out their hearts, raising their voices above the hubbub in an effort to be heard. This would build up into a frenzy with dancing and kicking up of heels in between shouts of exultation.

These rumbustious goings-on raised eyebrows in some quarters, but as far as Billy was concerned the salvation of a sinner was good cause for celebration.

Billy now had an over-riding enthusiasm for life. The diminutive man's habit of scooping Joey up in his arms and twirling her around the living room was re-echoed in the chapel with saved sinners. This caused some folk to mutter 'I 'ope 'ee don' never do that t'me!' Joey used to complain that he would go through the floorboards if he didn't stop capering about – and then of course came the day that he did!

Billy particularly loved to recount one story about 'the lost frock'. It seems that he went to Truro to buy a new frock for his little daughter and after putting it in his basket he kicked up his heels and danced his way home. When his wife asked him where the frock was, he replied, 'Tis in the basket'. But when he realised that the basket was empty, he declared, 'Glory to God! I must've danced the frock out o' the basket on the way 'ome!' and thought it a great joke. After telling this story in the chapel the next day, he reached home to find that well-wishers had left enough money to buy a replacement. Not only that, but the finder of the frock returned it to him a few days later, which meant that the lucky little girl had two new frocks, and Billy leapt about crying 'Glory! Glory! Glory!'

A similar thing happened after the sole of one of his well worn boots came off, as he was walking along a muddy track. He held it on high, pointing out, 'I've wore out these 'ere boots in Thy cause, Father, an' I've got no money to buy new!' A few days later a friend invited him to accompany him to Truro, and bought him a new pair of boots and other clothing. Billy and his family were always short of money because he gave it away to those less fortunate than himself. He was so loved by his flock that someone usually came up trumps in these situations, thus strengthening his belief that the Lord would provide.

One of Billy's sternest critics was a former drinking partner from his Devonshire days, who had also seen the light but who favoured the rather more staid Wesleyan approach. He sometimes went along to the Bible Christian chapel for old time's sake, slinking out before the high jinks began in earnest. He told Billy that he could not stand all the commotion with everybody praying and shouting and cavorting around. 'Tis as noisy as an ale 'ouse on pay night!' he declared rather scornfully. But it seems he changed his tune after a dream demonstrating that he was foolish to condemn such jubilation. So he joined the Bible Christians, shouting and gyrating with the best of them.

Perhaps the conversion which gave our hero the most joy was that of the vicar of Baldhu, William Haslam, who recognised that these Cornish religious revivals awakened sinners and refreshed believers. William Haslam, an accomplished architect, who had always been an Anglo-Catholic in his belief and practices, was preaching in his church one Sunday, when a local Methodist preacher in the congregation suddenly jumped to his feet exclaiming, 'Praise the Lord! The Parson is converted!' As soon as Billy got wind of this switch to evangelicalism, he rushed off to the vicarage, arriving at breakfast time. When Haslam answered the door and confirmed that the entire household had been converted, Billy swept past him, singing and dancing with the three maids around the kitchen table, before returning to the dining room with the dazed vicar in his arms, and rolling on the floor in ecstasy.

Preachers, whose chapel congregations tended not to have much in the way of material possessions, but tried to look their best on Sundays, could be very harsh on anyone tempted by vanity to put on airs and graces or to try to follow fashion. Once when Billy was in full flow in the pulpit at St Blazey, some girls with imitation flowers in their bonnets were trying to suppress their mirth at his quaintness of expression. He rounded on them saying, 'Tis the likes of you I'm praichin' at, you gigglin' maidens down there weth th'devel's flowers in yer 'ats!' The former hard drinker and smoker disagreed with drinking and smoking and the growing of long beards, which came into fashion in his later years. When someone pointed out that they were natural, he retorted, 'An' do yer serpose that 'eaven ever meant for everything t'jus' stay natrel? Do yer prune yer fruit trees, or let 'un grow wild, jus' as they please?'

Billy's religious fervour wherever he was led to him being told, when down in the mines: 'We don't want no preachin' down 'ere. You preach where you're planned to, an' leave us alone. You go your way, an' leave us t'ours.' But Billy had no intention of confining his evangelistic activities to the pulpit, and continued to visit saints and sinners around the countryside. Not everyone welcomed his calls, and when he knocked on one cottage door a little girl opened it and told him, 'Mother's out.' Billy peered past her and noticed a pair of shoes protruding from beneath a billowing curtain drawn across a cupboard. Raising his bushy eyebrows knowingly he said, 'Aw, she's gone out,'as she? Well, nex' time she do go out, tell 'er ter take 'er feet with 'er, me 'andsome!'

In spite of the odd setback from critics, many folk still flocked to the meeting places to savour the Billy Bray experience. A popular story which went the rounds highlighted the occasion when he stood on a barrel to preach, but was jeered at by some on account of his wild antics in the name of religion. He responded by telling them that if he danced his way through the barrel, he would shout 'Hallelujah!' through the bunghole. Rather less well known were his faith healings, when long term sick folk metaphorically took up their beds and walked.

Billy had stood in the pulpit of many chapels since finding his fledgling feet at Hicks Mill, but he was most closely associated with three he built in his home area. The first was on a piece of land at Cross Lanes given to him by his mother, which he called Bethel, meaning a hallowed spot or House of the Lord. The second was at Kerley Downs. The problems encountered in building these chapels were attributed to 'Old Smutty Face', and the subsequent breakthroughs to divine intervention. Having built the second chapel he needed a pulpit, and thought he could adapt a three cornered cupboard he saw in a sale room. He could not believe it when he was outbid, but it eventually came his way when it turned out to be too big to get through the purchaser's doorway. The opening service was conducted by an educated minister, who lacked sparkle, and there was a general sigh of relief the following Sunday, when Billy appeared and injected life into the new building. The third chapel was at Carharrick, where a gentleman donated a piece of land, leaving Billy to overcome the enormous challenge of raising the money and acquiring the materials needed to construct a large, handsome chapel. He called it Great Deliverance, because its completion was a tremendous act of faith. (This chapel has since been pulled down and a group of modern houses known as Billy Bray's Mews now occupies the site.)

As he grew older, Billy felt increasingly confident that 'Father' was always by his side, and that heaven was home. His unswerving faith brought great comfort to others, particularly when he visited the sick and dying. Even his critics would summon him on their deathbeds. When a vicar once expressed admiration for his unshakable faith, Billy said that it had not always been easy, but that he had the advantage of not being cluttered by book learning.

Billy was a great source of strength to his beloved wife, Joey, through a long and painful illness, and when she died he was joyful that she had gone on to better things. Even in his old age he walked vast distances to the Sunday services instead of taking a donkey cart as he did on any other day, for he was a strict

Billy Bray's 'Three Eyes' chapel at Kerley Downs, whose construction around 1835 was an act of faith. (Sheila Bird)

Sabbatarian. By this time he had returned to his home area, and when his health deteriorated and he became too weak to go out saving souls, his old associates visited him in his cottage, where his words of wit and wisdom continued to be punctuated by loud and enthusiastic exultations. As his life began to ebb away, his doctor was much moved when Billy asked him, 'When I get to heaven shall I give 'em your compliments, and tell 'em that you be comin' too?' The last word he uttered, in a strong, firm voice was 'Glory!' He died on 25th May 1868.

A granite obelisk in the churchyard at Baldhu and the chapels which remain in the landscape serve to remind us of Billy Bray, the miners' preacher, whose enduring reputation spread far beyond Cornwall, and who might be regarded by some as 'St Billy of Baldhu'.

5

Dolly Pentreath 1692–1777

The Last Speaker of the Cornish Language?

> *The principal love and knowledge of this (the Cornish) language lived in 'Dr Kenall the Civilian', and with him lieth buried; for the English speech doth still encroach upon it, and hath driven the same into the uttermost skirts of the shire.*
>
> (Richard Carew: *Survey of Cornwall*, 1602)

The colourful fishwife Dolly Pentreath of Mousehole, who died in 1777, was a legend in her own lifetime and the legend has gained momentum ever since. She is remembered not so much for any heroic deeds but for championing the Cornish language and everything the Cornish stood for. Dolly took some intriguing secrets with her to the grave and has remained something of an enigma ever since.

The Cornish language started to go into decline when the New English Prayer book was introduced at the time of the Reformation. English was a language that few in Cornwall understood, and, despite protests from the Cornish people, who wanted to stick to their old religion and familiar rituals, they were obliged to accept the new prayer book, which the authorities refused to have translated into Cornish. Thus the English language crept into common usage via the churches, taking longer to reach the remoter areas and the far west. The old Cornish language remained in use amongst the fisherfolk and tinners of the parishes of Paul and St Just, and when the evangelist John Wesley and his followers ventured across the Tamar as late as 1743, they felt as if they had entered a foreign land.

DOLLY PENTREATH 1692–1777

Shrewd Dolly Pentreath was ahead of her time in recognising the potential of tourism and promoting an interest in the old Cornish language. (Sheila Bird collection)

Dolly was a fisherman's daughter, brought up in a traditional, Cornish speaking family, and it was not until she was a young woman hawking heavy loads of fish around the countryside and needing to be understood by her customers that she started to speak English. At least that's what Dolly told visitors to Mousehole.

There was great competition amongst the women whose task it was to sell the catches, and an ability to cry their wares in sonorous tones and indulge in a persuasive line of patter would be reflected in their takings after the toil of the day. These tough women transported incredibly heavy loads of fish around a large area, in specially fashioned baskets or cowals, which were supported on their backs with broad bands passing across their foreheads and through their traditional headgear. After many years of selling fish, it was not surprising that poor old Dolly's back became troublesome and at such times she was obliged to seek help from the parish. But, being of a proud and independent nature, Dolly made every effort to generate her own income, and, like many another doughty dame with a colourful disposition, she hit upon the idea of becoming a white witch.

In those days country folk had great faith in the multi-talented claims of white witches or pellars, who would perambulate the countryside, curing all ills and freeing innocent folk and their animals from evil spells cast by black witches, if the price was right. Dolly created her own mystical style by muttering in old Cornish interspersed with a load of mumbo jumbo and concocting magic spells.

Although Dolly may have been small in stature, she more than made up for it in personality. She was no shrinking violet and had a voice which re-echoed for miles around. She could smoke a pipe, down a flagon of ale and let forth a stream of colourful invectives along with the best of them. This extrovert, artful old dame was ahead of her time when it came to spotting the potential of self-promotion, and exploiting the naivety of others.

She became a well-known figure throughout the area, capitalising on being regarded as a lovable eccentric, proficient in the old Cornish language. She also fostered the larger than life legends which surrounded her – and, it seems, had a fixation about mirrors. On entering a room where a looking glass was suspended she would get all excited and exclaim, 'Aw, what a fine, pretty little room you have in theer!' Was this an excuse to admire her own reflection, or to enhance her magical reputation?

Her most daring exploit was probably the hiding of a fugitive up her commodious chimney.

Dolly lived in a cottage near the quay, which had a chimney with a very large cavity, convenient for the storing of illicit goods. The story goes that, as she was sitting by the open door one fine day, a man suddenly appeared and rushed into her cottage, saying that the ship's officers were after him and would hang him from the yard-arm if they caught him. This was a situation after Dolly's own heart, so she popped the desperate naval deserter up the chimney without further ado. Just to be sure not to arouse any suspicion, the quick-witted dame grabbed an armful of dried furze, and started a fire in the wide open grate. Then she placed a crock on the hob to boil, and a large kieve (copper vat) in the centre of the kitchen, which she used for washing. By the time a naval officer and his men burst into the kitchen, Dolly was innocently sitting on a stool, with her bare legs dangling over the kieve, apparently waiting for the water to boil.

Had she seen a man on the run? The very idea! And she just a poor old woman waiting for the water to heat up to bathe her weary feet. The intruders were all very welcome to wash their feet after all that rushing about. They politely declined the offer, but explained that they were obliged to make a search of the house in the course of their duties. Why not take a look in the crock to see if he was hiding in there? suggested Dolly sarcastically, and the hitherto meek and mild old lady started to show her true colours. As the naval men took a look around, Dolly rattled away in an unfamiliar and rather unladylike language, increasing the volume after hearing a stifled cough from the direction of the chimney. Attack being the best means of defence, the old battleaxe let rip, shouting and screaming and throwing her stout shoes and other handy missiles at the hapless officers, before reaching for the wood chopper and rushing outside to tell the world that they were harassing a poor, defenceless old woman.

Discretion being the better part of valour, the naval men took to their heels and were relieved to return to the safety of the warship anchored out in Mount's Bay. Dolly released the wanted man, who slipped out of harbour aboard a fishing lugger bound that night for Guernsey, where deserters, debtors and other refugees sought safety.

Dolly revelled in all the publicity generated by her antics. She thought she had really made it when the Hon. Daines Barrington, brother of Captain, later Admiral, Barrington, turned up in 1768. Barrington was on a visit to Cornwall to ascertain whether the Cornish language was still being spoken. He was directed to Mousehole by a Penzance landlord, who told him that an old fish jouster called Dolly Pentreath was wont to lapse into an unknown tongue with her cronies when the price he offered did not meet with her approval. On his arrival in Mousehole, Barrington adopted a provocative approach, declaring he had laid a wager that there was no one left who could converse in Cornish. This challenge prompted the indignant Dolly to jabber away for several minutes in a language which resembled Welsh. Daines Barrington could hardly believe his luck in finding a living speaker of Cornish, in view of the fact that the great antiquarian scholar William Borlase, who lived at Ludgvan, had stated 14 years earlier that the language had 'altogether ceased'.

Daines Barrington never returned to Cornwall, but further enquires about the old fish jouster a few years later brought forth a letter from a gentleman residing nearby, the contents of which were published in the learned journal *Archaeologia* in 1776. The letter stated that Dolly was now a little deaf and bent with old age, but was still able to walk three miles to Castle Horneck and back, whatever the weather, and had a good memory. She insisted that she could not speak a word of English until she was over 20, explaining that her fisherman father sent her to Penzance to sell fish when she was 12; there she spoke Cornish and was understood by most of the local population and even the gentry. She was proud of the fame she had achieved as a speaker of Cornish and liked to recall the visit of a gentleman a few years before, in regard to this. By this time she had evidently established herself as the very last speaker of the Cornish language in her own mind, for the letter went on to say, 'She is positive that there is neither in Mousehole nor in any other part of the country, any other person who knows anything of it, or, at least can converse in it.' The letter concluded by saying that she was poor, and maintained partly by the parish. She was making ends meet by fortune telling and 'gabbling Cornish'.

Some local people made fun of poor old Dolly and her linguistic exploits but they never achieved enduring fame, as she did. Daines Barrington's claim of discovering a Cornish speaking character was met with scepticism by his sophisticated colleagues in London, and it became something of a joke. However, the publicity thus engendered had a more positive spin-off in West Cornwall, in that it led to her portrait being painted by the budding young Cornish artist John Opie, whose patron was Sir John St Aubyn of St Michael's Mount, and the portrait still adorns the walls of the castle on top of St Michael's Mount to this day.

Having laid his research before the Society of Antiquaries, Mr Barrington had hopes of getting a Welsh linguist to visit the old dame of Mousehole, in an attempt to save the last vestiges of the dying language. Unfortunately this never happened, and Dolly died in 1777, her age unknown. Dolly was buried in Paul churchyard, just up the hill from Mousehole. The undertaker was George Badcock, and eight pall-bearers were chosen to take the local heroine to her final resting place. Half way up the steep hill they paused, protesting that they would not budge another inch without taking some suitable liquid refreshment. The coffin was deposited in a by lane while one of them went to fetch a bottle of gin. Having knocked back the contents and enjoyed a philosophical discussion about life in general, they marched the old lady off with every solemnity.

A year after Dolly's death Mr Thomas, a mining engineer of Truro, wrote an epitaph in Cornish, which in translation began:

Old Dolly Pentreath a hundred and two,
Dead and buried in Paul parish.

But it was never inscribed on her tombstone, for none had been set up at the time of her death. This epitaph rhymed in Cornish, but not in its English translation, which prompted a certain Mr Collins to adapt it to the more familiar version 11 years later:

Old Doll Pentreath, one hundred aged and two,
Deceased and buried in Paul parish too.

The notion that Dolly was a centenarian seems to have originated in the original Cornish verse.

The knowledge of this epitaph prompted many to search in vain for the celebrated lady's tombstone in Paul churchyard. This led to a desire for one to be erected and, when it happened in 1860, it was at the behest of the Reverend John Garrett, an Irishman who was a newcomer to the parish, and the Frenchman Prince Louis Lucien Bonaparte, a nephew of the first Napoleon, who had an interest in languages. The monument was erected with great ceremony, but unfortunately it was to cause controversy on account of being placed in the wrong position,

Dolly Pentreath's memorial set in the wall of Paul churchyard.
(Sheila Bird collection)

and erroneously stating that Dolly died in 1778. This gave rise to a popular belief that Dolly's departed spirit would haunt the churchyard until the memorial was placed where her bones lay. The artful old dame would have been tickled pink to know that she was still stirring things up nearly a century after her death.

Many local folk claimed to have knowledge of the whereabouts of Dolly's grave, but Bernard Victor's grandfather George Badcock, who had made her pinewood coffin and been the undertaker at her funeral, had shown him exactly where she was buried between two elm trees. Bernard Victor explained all this to various influential personalities over the years, and his perseverance finally led to the re-inscribed stone being repositioned on 17th August 1887, 110 years after her death. A large crowd gathered to witness this strange happening, carried out by Mr J.S. Tregenza and his men, under the direction of Bernard Victor. Mr Baily of nearby Lynwood was also there in his capacity as a member of the Penzance Natural History and Antiquarian Society, and he documented details of the necessary exhumation, with the intention of presenting his findings to the Society the following year. Having breached the churchyard wall to erect the monument, they came upon Dolly's skeleton inside the worm-eaten remains of a pitch pine coffin between the interlacing roots of the old elm trees. The skull attracted great attention in regard to its strange shape and bony prominences between the eye sockets. Such thickening of the skull is now attributed to a painful condition known as Paget's disease. Three of her teeth remained intact.

Intrusion into the poor old soul's post-mortal privacy did not stop there, for the exhumation threw up other conundrums. According to the parish records of Paul, it was Dolly Jeffery who was buried on 27th December 1777, not Dolly Pentreath, and there were no centenarians of either name in that parish during the 18th century. It was suggested that Pentreath was Dolly Jeffery's maiden name, but there is no record of such a marriage.

DOLLY PENTREATH 1692–1777

Expert investigations into the Pentreath family ancestry came upon a Dorothy Pentreath, who was baptised in 1714, with a mother of the same name, but she would have been only 63 in 1777. The most likely contender was a Doaryte Pentreath, daughter of Nicholas Pentreath, baptised in May 1692. She would have been 85 in 1777, but looking older on account of her medical condition. Her father and her eldest brother were called Nicholas, which ties in with a six lined verse in the old Cornish language, about a man of that name who continually refused to pay his fish tithes. The mystery deepens with the parish register recording the baptism of John, the illegitimate son of Dolly Pentreath, on 18 October 1729, when Doaryte would have been 37, and there is speculation as to whether the father's name was Jeffery.

Some Cornish was still being spoken at the time of Dolly's death, although she maintained that she was the last to have been brought up speaking the language exclusively. There is a plaque on the wall of Zennor church, which cites two John Daveys, father and son (1770–1884 and 1812–1891), who are buried in the churchyard, as being the last to understand the Cornish language. Be that as it may, the colourful folk heroine of Mousehole has done much to promote Cornwall, its unique culture and the revival of the old Cornish language.

6

Richard Trevithick 1771–1833

Saluting 'Cap'n Dick'

The child born to Richard and Anne Trevithick on 13th April 1771, at Pool in the parish of Illogan, was destined to change the world. He was instrumental in the progress and design of steam-driven transport during the Industrial Revolution and built and drove the first successful railway locomotive in the world. This feat was not fully acknowledged until 2004 when the Royal Mint struck a £2 coin to celebrate the bi-centenary of the first high pressure steam engine to run effectively on metal rails. It depicts Trevithick's locomotive, and the words 'R. Trevithick . . . 1804 . . . Invention . . . Industry . . . Progress . . . 2004' around the edge.

As the only boy in a family of five children, young Richard was his mother's pet, and his schoolmaster complained that he was a disobedient, slow, obstinate, spoiled boy, who was very inattentive and frequently played truant. When he was in school, he would sit on his own and draw lines and figures on his slate instead of attending to his lessons. However, he had an intuitive grasp of mathematics, swiftly arriving at the correct answer without going through any calculations in the usual way. This uncanny gift was to serve him well throughout his life,

A £2 coin was minted to mark the 200th anniversary of Trevithick building the first self-propelled railway locomotive.

and was the first indication of his genius. When chided by his teacher for not solving mathematical problems in the way he had been taught, he retorted arrogantly, 'I'll do six sums to your one!' His inventiveness was reflected in his novel spelling, a trait which remained with him for life.

The young prodigy's birthplace lay in the heartland of Cornwall's mining country, close to the legendary mines of Dolcoath (where his father was mine captain), Cook's Kitchen, Pool, Tin Croft and Roskear, at a time of great opportunity for gifted engineers with inventive minds.

After leaving school he was a bit of a rebel, preferring to wander around the engine houses and underground galleries on his own, instead of sitting in his father's office learning about mine administration and finance. His father was dismayed at his wayward son's apparently aimless behaviour, but in reality the youngster was observing and educating himself in his own way, and surprising others by solving problems which had eluded the highly qualified experts. Then, to his father's astonishment Richard was given a responsible position as engineer in a neighbouring mine, having gained the confidence and respect of the mine captain. Thus, at the age of 19, 'RT' was commanding a salary of 30 shillings a month at Eastern Stray Park Mine, which was a very substantial amount in those days.

By this time the fair haired, sturdy and rather thick set, blue eyed boy had grown into a fine figure of a man. He was six foot two, broad shouldered and extremely strong and genial and easy going, with a good sense of humour and a ready smile, which lit up his handsome face. He was also impetuous and quick tempered. If anyone got on the wrong side of him, he would threaten to throw him down the nearest mine shaft.

It was part of the culture in those days for young miners to engage in competitive feats of strength, and he astonished everyone with his ability to lift heavy weights. He used to stand at the top of a mine swinging a sledge-hammer above his head

Richard Trevithick. (Cornish Studies Library, The Cornwall Centre)

to get a bit of exercise, and on one occasion, when some miners were attempting to throw a heavy sledge-hammer across the yard, he grabbed it and hurled it right over the roof of the engine house. He could write his name on a beam six foot off the ground with his arm fully extended and a 56lb weight suspended from his thumb. RT certainly made his mark on one occasion. After one of the monthly shareholders' dinners at Dolcoath Mine, he grabbed a sturdy engineer called Hodge around the waist and swung him all over the place, leaving the imprint of his boots on the ceiling!

RT had entered the world as the Industrial Revolution in the Midlands and the North was shifting the emphasis from an agricultural to an industrial economy. In Cornwall, mining had reached a stage where the readily accessible tin, lead and copper lodes had been worked out, and there was a pressing need to obtain these minerals at ever deepening levels. Apart from the obvious hazards of working deeper underground, there was the problem of getting rid of the water which accumulated in the workings. This was the necessity which proved to be the mother of invention, and various pumps were designed, harnessing man-power, animal-power, water and wind-power. Thomas Savary, a Devon man, had produced a simple steam pump, known as the Miners' Friend. Then came the breakthrough of Thomas Newcomen's steam engine, which was actually driven by the pressure of the atmosphere and not by steam, and James Watt's pumping engine, which was a true steam engine. It derived its power from the vacuum created below the piston, and not from the pressure and expansion of the steam above.

RT was six years old when James Watt travelled down from the famous Soho works in Birmingham to supervise the installation of the first Boulton & Watt pumping engines at Wheal Busy, near Chacewater, and Ting Tang, near Redruth. They had been built in Cornwall with some small parts supplied from Birmingham, and an annual premium was to be paid for their use. James Watt and

Richard Trevithick Senior did not hit it off, and this uneasy relationship led to a desire to produce a better design in Cornwall.

A few years later, RT was working on the plunger pole pump, a simple and practical device to be used in conjunction with a beam engine, which was a great improvement on previous designs and soon came into widespread use. He also reversed the plunger pole pump, turning it into a water power engine, and introduced the egg-shaped iron bucket known as a kibbal, for raising ore up the mineshafts. His engine-building projects took him frequently to John Harvey's foundry at Hayle, where he met and fell in love with Harvey's statuesque and striking daughter Jane. He was commanding a good salary as an engineer at this time, and after his father's death in 1797 his financial position became more secure, so the handsome couple married at St Erth parish church that November, when the rising star was 26. It was a good match, for Jane was a loyal and understanding wife, with an independent streak and great strength of character. She bore him two daughters and four sons, one of whom became Locomotive Superintendent of the London and North Western Railway, and wrote a comprehensive book about his remarkable father.

While in London to sit in on a legal case involving the infringement of copyright by a rebel employee who had defected to Cornwall, RT met fellow Cornishman Davies Gilbert, a wealthy landowner. Gilbert was a prominently political man of a scientific and mathematical bent and destined to become President of the Royal Society. He recognised the exceptional talent in the young Trevithick and was to become his friend, mentor and sounding-board.

RT's marriage marked the beginning of the most inventive period of his life. He achieved an incredible range of engineering accomplishments, but his most important work was on the high pressure steam engine and the locomotive, which he began by making experimental models.

The first steam vehicle had actually been created by a Frenchman back in 1763, and it was a rather clumsy looking three-wheeled tractor. There were many technical problems, and it crashed during the trial. So the project was abandoned. RT produced Britain's first full-sized locomotive in Camborne in 1801, which was designed to run on the road. There was great excitement that Christmas when they took her on a trial run, in an event that became immortalised in the folk song:

Going up Camborne Hill, coming down,
Going up Camborne Hill, coming down;
The horses stayed still, the wheels went around,
Going up Camborne Hill, coming down!

And indeed, horse-drawn vehicles came to a standstill, and everyone gazed in amazement at the noisy and thrilling spectacle, the like of which had never been seen before.

The locomotive had been a natural progression from RT's fast winding engines harnessing high pressure steam, which came to be known as Puffers on account of the evocative noise they made as they exhausted directly into the atmosphere. Equipping the Puffers with wheels and allowing them to propel themselves would prove more cost-effective and efficient in moving from one mine to another. Harvey's started to cast the iron parts in 1800, and a wealth of local talent including RT's cousin Andrew Vivian, Arthur Woolf and Nicholas Holman was involved, while Davies Gilbert assisted with practical experiments in regard to iron-tyred wheels to grip the road surface.

Adrenalin must have been flowing freely on that cold and wet Christmas Eve, as the little locomotive was hauled onto the highway outside Jonathan Tyack's smithy, where she had been assembled. After getting up steam, she set off down the hill with RT at the steering tiller, and men and miners leaping onto the footplate to provide extra weight and grip as her wheels slipped and spun on the stones and mud. The eight or nine men providing stability clung on for dear life as the innovative Puffer lurched and skidded along the slippery surface at about seven miles an hour in the driving rain, which eventually started to cool the boiler and caused the steam pressure to fall. RT and his team turned her round and retreated to Knapp's Hotel at the bottom of Tehidy Road, where they dried out their clothes and took some refreshment before returning the mobile Puffer to Tyack's smithy for the night. A plaque was later erected in memory of Richard Trevithick, 'to commemorate the site where the first locomotive engine was assembled by him and from where it was started on its highly successful run to Beacon Hill, Christmas Eve 1801'.

On Christmas Day they took the locomotive through Camborne to visit Andrew Vivian's family at Crane Manor, causing some to marvel in wonder and others to quake with fear. One old lady was heard to declare, 'Good gracious, whatever next! Tis like a puffin' Devil!' And this affectionate name has remained ever since. On Boxing Day the Puffing Devil took to the highway once more, heading for Tehidy, where Lord and Lady de Dunstanville and Davies Gilbert were waiting eagerly to savour RT's latest invention. However, the wet weather had affected the road surface, and she lurched over as her front wheels struck a gully and the tiller was torn from Andrew Vivian's grasp. RT and his gang pushed her under a roadside shelter before adjourning to Knapp's Hotel again and drowning their sorrows with a drink or two and a hearty meal of roast goose. They must have had a good time, for they forgot about their precious engine, whose boiler ran dry, became red hot and caused a fire which destroyed the locomotive and the shelter.

The sculptor L. E. Merrifield's bronze statue outside Camborne public library, depicting RT in tailcoat and breeches, looking up Beacon Hill, clasping a steam locomotive in one hand and a pair of dividers in the other, symbolises his achievements and the dramatic happenings here that Christmas. Replicas of the Puffing

RICHARD TREVITHICK 1771–1833

This statue of Richard Trevithick stands outside the library at Camborne. (Sheila Bird)

Devil and subsequent steam powered vehicles have been an essential part of Camborne's Trevithick Day celebrations in April for many years.

RT and Andrew Vivian took out a patent incorporating the features of the Puffing Devil and other machines. Although another road carriage was produced in 1803, making a number of journeys around London, it failed to attract media attention, so RT concentrated on fulfilling the huge demand for high pressure stationary engines for a variety of purposes. He sold a share of the patent for these machines to Samuel Homfray, an iron-master of Penydarren in South Wales, in 1803. Had he been more businesslike in his affairs, he would have been a wealthier man.

In the late 18th century, when the iron industry of South Wales was booming, a canal was built from Merthyr Tydfil to the docks at Cardiff, but as it became increasingly congested a railway was constructed between the Penydarren ironworks and Abercynon, using horse-power. RT was invited to Penydarren by Mr Homfray, who had bet a neighbouring iron-master 500 guineas even money that a steam locomotive could haul 10 tons of iron on the nine and three quarter miles from there to Abercynon.

His rival had mocked the whole idea of a steam locomotive, saying that iron wheels on iron rails would simply spin around, and nothing would happen. RT was to prove him wrong on 13th February 1804, thereby ushering in a new age of mass transportation.

RT continued to design road and railway locomotives, but the Catch-me-who-can, built in London in 1808, was to be his last locomotive. The restless genius then threw himself into a host of ingenious, widely ranging projects, mostly based on stationary high pressure engines. These could be applied to such tasks as crushing stone, boring brass cannon, powering mills, forging hammers, as well as driving paddle-wheel barges and dredgers. His work was to take him far from Cornwall. He was employed

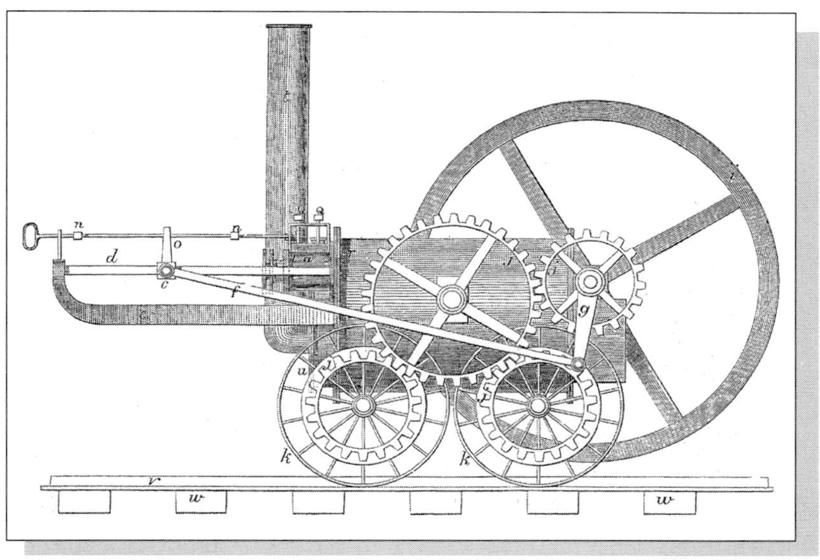

The first tram road locomotive made its inaugural trip from Penydarren to Abercynon in South Wales in 1804. (Cornish Studies Library, The Cornwall Centre)

by the Thames Archway Company, who were experiencing problems in driving a tunnel under the Thames. As it turned out Sir Marc Isambard Brunel and his son Isambard were to enjoy the triumph of completing the first tunnel under the Thames.

RT persuaded his wife and family to join him in London, but their two and a half years there were not very happy and they longed for Cornwall. He produced a seemingly endless catalogue of novel inventions before opting for a life of adventure in South America, working in the Peruvian silver mines, Costa Rica and far beyond. He moved his family back to Penzance, and sailed from there on 20th October 1816. The bells of Camborne church peeled out a welcome on his return eleven years later, but our hero had no business sense, did not always get his inventions properly patented, and died penniless at Dartford in Kent on 22nd April 1833, where he was working at the time. He was buried in the churchyard there.

The Cornish inventor of the steam locomotive had never been motivated by money; it was his genius that drove him on. He had no financial or business sense and never got the recognition he deserved. At a time when his pioneering work might have brought him fame and fortune, he left the country in search of new challenges and adventures, leaving Stephenson and other engineers to take the initiative from him.

The achievements of 'Cap'n Dick' were celebrated with great enthusiasm in Wales where they re-enacted that first railway journey from Penydarren to Abercynon, on the 200th anniversary. They re-dedicated RT's monument at Pontmorlais with its model locomotive and plinth adorned with the flag of St Piran. The band played as the train, drawn by its Type 37 locomotive, pulled into Merthyr Station, packed with railway enthusiasts. It was greeted by a large crowd of onlookers. Pop music impresario Pete Waterman, who had been a fireman before steam gave way to diesel, named the locomotive 'Richard Trevithick'. The day of jubilation culminated with a gala evening at Cyfarthfa Castle, and it was said of these celebrations for 'Cornwall's greatest son' that 'Wales has really done him proud'.

The then Transport Minister saluted RT's genius, and summed up his achievements by saying, 'What he did was set off a train of events that spread like wildfire across the world. The journey near Merthyr Tydfil kick-started the Industrial Revolution and transformed Wales and the world.'

7

Robert Stephen Hawker 1803–1875

The Creator of the Cornish 'National Anthem'

A good sword and a trusty hand,
A merry heart and true,
King James's men shall understand
What Cornish lads can do.
And have they fixed the where and when,
And shall Trelawny die?
Then twenty thousand Cornish men
Will know the reason why!
What! Will they scorn Tre, Pol and Pen,
And shall Trelawny die?
Then twenty thousand Cornish men
Will know the reason why!

The eccentric poet-parson of Morwenstow, Robert Stephen Hawker, who created the stirring ballad *Trelawny*, did much to promote the Cornish culture, and became an essential part of it himself. The boy was very much father-of-the-man, and, while some of his colourful characteristics may have been inherent, his boyhood experiences influenced his behaviour throughout the various stages of his life.

A look at our hero's family and inherited characteristics will give a greater understanding of the man he was to become. Hawker came from a family of medical men and men of the cloth, who tended to be extrovert and play prominent roles in public life. His grandfather Robert Hawker had been a 'frivolous, gay and thoughtless' youth, who got married at the age of 19 and went to Oxford. He apparently changed his spots after becoming incumbent of the Charles Church in Plymouth, where he was noted for his eloquent preaching, and developed into a prolific writer. Dr Hawker's doctrine was such that he saw social upheavals of the time as signs that the end of the world was nigh. He was so concerned about the plight of the poor and their physical and spiritual well-being, that his benevolent activities caused hardship for his own family.

Hawker's father, Jacob, initially became a surgeon in Plymouth, and married Jane Elizabeth Drewitt, a woman of delicate health, who nonetheless bore him nine children. The future parson of Morwenstow, and prolific writer of verse, was their first born, making his entry into the world on 3rd December 1803. Jacob Hawker, a rather quiet man, somewhat overshadowed by his flamboyant father and elder brother, decided to swap medicine for the church, and served at Altarnun as a curate before moving

The vicarage at Morwenstow, built by Hawker, is a fine edifice with a distinctive array of chimneys. (Cornish Studies Library, The Cornwall Centre)

on to Stratton, near Bude, where he eventually became the vicar. There had always been financial concerns, and the bright young lad was put in the care of his grandparents in Plymouth, where his kindly disposed Aunt Mary helped to pay for his education.

Young Hawker did not react too well to the strict regime of his grandfather's devout and evangelistic household, although the influence of his chiliastic ideology and the charitable treatment of the poor and suffering emerged in later years. He had an aversion to the pious ladies who swarmed around his grandfather and thought up some cunning ruses to frighten them off. He developed a penchant for reckless escapades and surprisingly brutal hoaxes and practical jokes during his time in Plymouth and back home in Stratton, where he spent his vacations. He enjoyed playing ghostly pranks, and his tricks included sending bogus orders of unwanted goods to people's homes (including a coffin) and painting the surgeon's horse with stripes like a zebra before summoning him with urgency to a distant house to make him look a fool. On one occasion he ran an enormous ball of string around the streets of Stratton, tripping people up.

One of his more amusing antics involved impersonating a mermaid on the rocks at Bude in the moonlight, combing his long seaweed locks, flashing a mirror about and singing a mournful dirge. This created quite a sensation for several consecutive nights, until the hoarse, shivering prankster wound up the performance with a rendition of the national anthem and disappeared into the waves. When he was not venting his frustration on everyone else, the lad tended to withdraw into a world of his own. He was a poet and dreamer by nature, and enjoyed reading books and appreciated the wonders of the natural world. His favourite book was *The Arabian Nights*, and he enjoyed Shakespeare, Scott and most of the classics. Hawker was moved by the sight of the relentless sea, the sound of the wind and the graceful forms of trees and vegetation, and fancied he saw images which inspired him to verse.

The promising lad was reluctant to take advantage of his educational opportunities. He resented scholastic discipline, and never achieved much in his time at Liskeard Grammar School. After leaving there at the age of 16 he worked briefly for a solicitor in Plymouth, then went on to the long established but run down Cheltenham Grammar School, where he became more focused, setting his sights on becoming a clergyman. He continued to write romantic poetry, inspired by his literary heroes, and eventually gained himself a place at Oxford University. His father had moved to Altarnun when he was a young child, and at that time he had got to know the family of Colonel Wrey L'ans, who spent part of the year at Efford Manor in Bude, where Hawker was always a welcome guest. He shared the family's love of literature and enjoyed browsing in their comprehensive library. He was also influenced by the Colonel's concern about the plight of victims of shipwreck, and the proper regulation of the salvaging of cargoes.

Colonel L'ans had died in 1816, leaving four daughters, and before going up to Oxford Hawker married the attractive, cultured and charming Charlotte L'ans, who had an annuity of about £200 a year, and a good sense of humour. The handsome, flamboyant and engaging bridegroom was 20 and his educated, well-preserved bride 41 but despite their unconventional age difference they enjoyed common interests and it turned out to be a loving and caring relationship.

Hawker went to Magdalen Hall, Oxford, in 1824, as a married undergraduate. There his studies between those centuries old cloistered walls were punctuated with champagne breakfasts, jolly japes and a gay and extravagant social life. The fact that Hawker also entertained the two older L'ans sisters caused some amusement, earning him the nickname, 'the man with three wives'.

The undergraduate from Cornwall continued to enjoy practical jokes. One of his student pranks involved poor old Nanny Heale, who lived in a hovel at the foot of a steep embankment on the outskirts of town, where nosey passers-by could peer down her chimney and see what she was up to. On one occasion they saw her crouching over the smoking embers, where a round crock filled with potatoes was suspended. So they dangled a rope down the chimney and hauled it up, causing the simple soul to exclaim, 'Massy 'pon my soul! Art gawn off, taties an' all?' The vessel was then deposited at the front door with a knock to gain her attention. She stumbled out and greeted the penitent crock with joy. 'So then! Theer't come back to holt, then! Ay, 'tis a cold out o' doors!'

The Hawkers spent the university vacations at the L'ans family home at Whitstone near Holsworthy, or at Ivy Cottage, near Bude, where the budding clergyman enjoyed being alone on the clifftop, communing with God and nature. He built himself a timber retreat in the woods at Whitstone, where he did a lot of reading and composed a number of ballads based on Cornish legends, which were published in *Records of the Western Shore* in 1832.

One of his Oxford chums, Francis Jeune, who was later to become a bishop, went to stay with them in Cornwall during the long summer vacation of 1825, when the two high spirited young men rode over to Boscastle on two 'Galloway nags', as recounted in Hawker's *Footprints of Former Men in Cornwall*. Having descended the dramatic steep valley from the north and been enchanted by the quaint old fashioned cottages clinging to the hillsides, they reached the harbour where the model of an old sailing vessel swinging above a doorway attracted their attention to the Ship Inn. They were greeted by the ample, ruddy faced hostess, Joan Treworgy, who had been born in the cottage next-door-but-one and had never travelled further than Forrabury church, where she was married. She summoned a scruffy lad called Tim to look after the Cap'ns' horses, instructing him to give them plenty of oats. Widow Treworgy saluted all the travellers in reasonably presentable attire as Cap'n, on the assumption that they were seafarers or officials from the mines and quarries, where this term was generally recognised.

The travellers were ushered into the cosy parlour, where they asked if they might have two beds for the night. They were informed that visitors were expected to sleep two in a bed, but if they insisted on having a bed each, the charge would have to be sixpence apiece. The evening meal would be a wholesome 'meat and taties'. 'Some call 'em purtaties,' said the hostess, 'but we always say taties 'ere.' She refused to be drawn on the type of meat on offer, merely repeating, 'meat – nice wholesome meat and taties!'

They sat down and speculated about the origins of the flabby, boneless roast meal they were consuming, wondering whether it might be a piece of Boscastle baby. Many years later Hawker was horrified to read in an old guidebook that 'the sillie people of Bouscastle and Boussinny do catch in the summer seas divers young soyles (seals), which, doubtful if they be fish or flesh, conynge (cunning) housewives will nevertheless roast, and do make thereof very savoury meat'.

Later that evening the two friends scrambled up a cabin ladder to a little bedroom, and when they opened the tiny casement window found that the general atmosphere was heavy with a smell of onions and cheese. They did not get much sleep that night, and in the early morning they ventured out to get some fresh air and enjoy the spectacular scenery from the heights. Hawker was moved by the sight of a sloop at anchor in the creek, with its mast and rigging 'like a network traced upon the morning sky'. The air became fresher as they reached the clifftop and beheld a scene which was 'exhilarating, stately and grand'.

This trip, made after he had spent some time in Oxford, heightened Hawker's awareness of the wonder and drama of the Cornish landscape, its romantic history and legends, and served to focus his literary aspirations on the characters and culture of the county. There was inspiration everywhere he looked. 'On the right-hand side and to the west, arose and stood the craggy heights of Dundagel (Tintagel), island and main, ennobled by the legends of old historic time. To the left, a boundless reach of granite-sprinkled moor, where barrow, logan rock, and cromlech stood, the mute memorials of Keltic antiquity. Beneath, and afar off, the sea, at that silent hour like some boundless lake . . . and at our feet the jumbled village crouching on either side of the steepy road, and clinging to its banks as if the inhabitants sought to secure access for escape when the earthquake should rend or the volcano pour . . .'

High spirits overtook the intellectual students from Oxford after this heady dawn experience. For on the steep descent to the village they noticed that every habitation had a pigsty, and, feeling sorry for the pent-up pigs, they decided to release them. Thereupon they careered down the hillsides en masse, 'as if with one hoof and mind'. The friends hastily returned to their attic room at the Ship, where their hostess and her household were asleep. The erupting crescendo of squealing and shouting eventually aroused them, and the miscreants requested some shaving water and feigned innocence as they asked what all the excitement was about. Then they went outside and watched the cottagers frantically trying to capture their pigs, feeling amused rather than guilty at having wreaked such havoc. The poor inhabitants thought they had been bewitched.

The adventurers asked for their ponies to be brought to the door, and requested a bill. Their hostess became very confused and flustered about this, and, after seeking the help of a neighbour, bustled in, bobbed a curtsy and pointed to some information chalked on the lid of the kitchen bellows, which read:

CAPTENS

T for 2	0	6
Sleep for 2	1	0
Meat & Taties & Beer	1	6
Bresks	1	6

They copied this out, paid up, and resumed their rural ride through the lanes of north Cornwall, laughing and joking about their exploits around Boscastle. The sometimes bizarre and paradoxical behaviour of our future hero-of-the-cloth, who thought that everyone else was a 'character', was destined to become absorbed into Cornish folklore making him one of the most colourful and eccentric characters of them all.

Young Hawker did not really apply himself conscientiously to his studies during the time he was at Oxford, although he managed to carry off the Newdigate Poetry Prize on the subject of Pompeii in 1827. He was too much of an individualist to accept the academic discipline of university life, preferring to do things in his own way, reading around the subject and producing a great deal of creative writing. His most famous and enduring ballad *The Song of the Western Men (Trelawny)* had already been published anonymously in 1825.

After gaining his degree in 1828, he became a deacon in 1829 and an ordained priest two years later.

Hawker initially served as a curate in the little village of North Tamerton, a few miles east of Whitstone, where the couple occupied a converted cottage in a moorland environment dotted with tumuli. The new curate would go around the parish with his well groomed and intelligent pet pig called Gyp. He was delighted when the Bishop of Exeter offered him the chance to become vicar of the bleak coastal parish of Morwenstow in 1834, with its towering cliffs and vulnerability to the relentless Atlantic storms. It was an ideal environment for this restless, creative free spirit.

Morwenstow lies in the far north of the county, with its high dramatic coastline on the western side, and is still a sparsely populated area characterised by rough moorland terrain, a network of fields, isolated farmsteads and small scattered settlements. The church town, consisting of the parish church of St Morwenna, the vicarage built by Hawker and the glebe farm, enjoys a unique and beautiful situation above an elongated, wooded gorge, dominated by towering cliffs on a section of coast notorious for shipwrecks in the days of sail. The name is thought to be have been derived from the saint to whom the church was dedicated, with the additional Anglo-Saxon 'stow'. According to legend (which may have been coloured up by Hawker), Morwenna was one of the 24 children of King Broccan of Breconshire, who watched the evening sun illuminate Henna Cliff across the water, and prayed that a church be established near 'yonder barbarous hill'. She was thought to have helped in the construction of the church, having indicated the correct position, carrying a stone for the font up from the shore on her head. Hawker believed in ghosts and claimed to have seen and spoken with the saint on a number of occasions. According to legend, her brother Necton arrived from Hartland and took her in his arms as she lay dying, to allow her to take one last, lingering look at her beloved Welsh homeland across the billowing waters of the Severn Sea.

Morwenstow had been without a vicar for a century before the earnest, idealistic young Hawker arrived on the scene. However, it soon became evident that the mellowed student prankster had met his match with his new found flock, whose souls he sought to save. Amongst the farmers, labourers, servants and traditional craftsmen in this harsh and isolated parish, there was a great deal of brutality and a hard core of smugglers, wreckers, religious dissenters and drunkards, and immorality was rife. They displayed hostility towards the personable, fresh faced newcomer, with humanitarian principles, who did all he could to win their hearts and minds, riding around the parish on his pony, visiting them all and taking note of their concerns. He was appalled by the poverty of the labourers, who lived in squalid conditions where pestilence was rife, and like his grandfather he championed their cause and became a hero in their eyes. Throughout his life his generosity was inclined to impinge on his own household.

On their arrival the Hawkers found the church in a very dilapidated condition, the vicarage had become a ruin and there was a pressing need for a new school. The problems of isolation and communication were compounded by the dangerous state of the ford at Coombe Valley on the road to Bude. Nothing daunted, the conscientious man of the cloth set about rectifying all this, endeavouring to raise money by subscription, but shouldering much of the expense himself. He had a bridge erected at Coombe, built a school in the centre of the parish at Shop, created a new vicarage and renovated the church. His impressive achievements made a positive impact on everyone's lives, but he said that everything he did was for the greater glory of God. He took an active part in the running of St Mark's School, where he delighted the pupils with colourful stories and legends about their environment, as well as giving them religious instruction. Although he was always regarded as an eccentric, his steadying influence on his wayward parishioners was beginning to take effect. Hawker's conversations with the older members of his flock provided lively and colourful material for his creative writing, giving us a rare insight into life in old Cornwall.

Hawker may have encouraged folk to keep on the straight and narrow, and been a good example to them in many ways, yet he liked to indulge his fads and fancies. He was a showman who enjoyed the limelight, yet a loner who valued his privacy. He was wont to take earnest scholars on an intellectual ride with exhibitions of deep mysticism. And, when folk asked a question he perceived to be silly, he could deflate them with his caustic wit. Although he was occasionally off-hand with the tourists, he was usually genial, generous and very hospitable to one and all.

Constructing the new vicarage gave him the opportunity to indulge his whims. The alterations he made during the restoration of the church, which were a puzzle to many, were steeped in obscure symbolism inspired by the scriptures and early Eastern church history. His personality was freely expressed

The Reverend Robert Stephen Hawker at the door of his vicarage in stylish ecclesiastical gear. (Cornish Studies Library)

in the lavish design of the vicarage, this imposing Victorian Gothic edifice, with its array of strange chimneys depicting church and college towers with which he had been associated. The kitchen chimney was fashioned to resemble his mother's tomb!

Having completed the project, Hawker, whose living here brought in a handsome £365 a year, had this verse inscribed in the stonework above the front door:

A House, A Glebe, A Pound a Day,
A pleasant Place to Watch and Pray;
Be true to Church, Be Kind to Poor,
O Minister, for evermore.

This drew forth the anonymous satirical riposte:

With all these benefits supplied,
A pound a day, and more beside,
How very good this man should prove,
How full of zeal, how full of love!

But different the times we see
Since Jesus walked on Galilee,
And did poor fishermen prepare
His holy Gospel to declare.

Nor purse nor scrip He bade them take,
But preach the Gospel for His sake,
And not a single word did say,
Of house, or glebe or pound a day!

The newly ordained vicar sought to brighten up the lives of his parishioners, focusing on the church festivals and introducing refreshing innovations. In this remote agricultural parish, where so much depended on a good harvest, he established the much loved harvest festival of thanksgiving. He made Christmas a more joyful occasion by decorating the church, ringing the bells and started the custom of carol singing around the villages. He introduced the tradition of nine lessons and carols.

In his life and his work, Hawker was inspired by nature and the stark beauty of the landscape of this harsh environment. Being a parson here was never easy, but the situation which caused him most distress and affected his physical and mental well-being was brought about by the wind, the weather, the unyielding nature of the shoreline and the prevailing currents, which deposited a horrifying catalogue of shipwrecks on his coastal doorstep. He dreaded the approach of storms and fancied he heard the desperate cry of a dying sailor in every gust of wind. For he was only too well aware of the old saying:

From Padstow Point to Lundy Light
Is a watery grave, by day or night.

On such occasions he did everything he could to help, and took responsibility for the survivors. When disaster struck it fell to him and his helpers to carry the bodies up from the shore to be deposited in a room at the vicarage until such time as the coroner had called and authorised their burial in the churchyard, where scores of them now lie. The sensitive, highly strung vicar lived in a state of anxiety about pending storms, which often left the Bristol Channel 'peopled with corpses', and which so often resulted in horribly bloated, decomposing bodies and body parts being strewn along this rocky shoreline. Hawker had experienced terrible nightmares about the wrecks and mangled corpses and had a fear of being haunted by the unburied dead. He hated taking burial services with the stench from decaying bodies, but nevertheless he had the courage and moral fibre to tackle such daunting tasks, treating the victims with reverence and giving them decent burials. In former times victims of shipwreck were unceremoniously cast into pits on the shore above the high water line.

The hardworking and caring parson's compassion also embraced the whole of the animal kingdom, all of which he believed possessed souls, and even wild creatures had a remarkable affinity with him. Hawker kept a number of pets, including nine cats, some of which were in the habit of following him around the parish, and even keeping him company in the pulpit. Visitors were most wary of a pet deer called Robin Hood, whose spirited antics stripped visiting clergymen of their dignity on various occasions. He was concerned about the welfare of donkeys employed to haul heavy goods up the steep, winding paths from ships wrecked on the shore, as authorised by the coastguards and shipping agents.

Harvesting the bounty of the sea had long been part of the culture for impoverished coastal communities, but Hawker had had a calming influence on some of the more brutal smuggling and wrecking activities around these parts. Nevertheless, the exploits of Cruel Coppinger, a Danish smuggler, and other colourful tales of derring-do became the inspiration for many of his romantic stories and ballads which have been handed down to us.

Hawker did most of his creative writing in a hut on the cliffside, which he had constructed himself from timber salvaged from ships wrecked on the shore below. Despite his dread of storms and shipwrecks, the sea in all its moods was a never-ending source of inspiration and wonder. The hideaway allowed him to escape into a mystical world of dreams, which helped him to cope with his traumatic experiences and found an outlet in his literary outpourings.

The need for some light relief from the grim realities of life found expression through his attire. Vanity must also have played a part in this, as he was well aware of his good looks and fine physique and liked to cut a dash. His religious philosophy and flamboyant dress was inspired by the eastern roots of the Cornish Church, and not by Rome. He hated black and said that he did not want to be mistaken for a waiter or an unemployed undertaker. His striking outfits ranged from the full regalia of brimless cap and cassock, in which he clambered over the rough terrain, to the later fisherman's jersey, black sea boots and three quarter length claret coloured coat, re-echoing the Biblical theme of being a fisher of men. A variety of useful accoutrements were attached to his person, including a pencil, with which he jotted down interesting ideas in a notebook, to be developed in due course.

Charlotte was a selfless, cheerful, good natured person, who played the supportive role of minister's wife with sensitivity and charm, and was popular with the parishioners. They were a devoted couple, and, when her health declined and her eyesight began to fail, her husband was loving and tender, and spent many hours reading to her in the vicarage or in his hut out on the cliffs. He was heartbroken when she died in February 1863, and found it very difficult to rebuild his life. He threw himself into his duties around the parish, sticking rigidly to his structured day and taking very little sleep. At this painful time he resorted to taking opium, which he had used spasmodically to ease his stress-related illnesses. The tragic year of Charlotte's death also saw a fire at the vicarage and two more shipwrecks during the stormy month of December. Yet this was the year of his greatest literary achievement in the writing of the epic poem *The Quest of the Sangraal*, inspired by Arthurian legend and full of striking imagery.

Just as the unconventional man of the cloth seemed set to mellow into a lonely existence in his twilight years, he met and fell in love with an attractive, intelligent, high spirited woman 40 years his junior, and found a new lease of life. Pauline Kuczynski, who was the daughter of an exiled Polish count and an English woman, came to Morwenstow while working as a governess for the family of a Yorkshire vicar who had acquired a holiday home here. The parishioners were delighted at the prospect of having a new lady to run the vicarage and look after the old boy, but Pauline's widowed mother and family were opposed to the match. Pauline insisted, however, that she would rather enjoy 10 years with the still handsome and personable Hawker than spend a lifetime with any other man. They were married in London on 21st December 1864, and he subsequently became the father of three daughters named Morwenna, Rosalind and Juliot. The couple were well matched, and his happiness inspired a renewed burst of writing activity. But as the years went by the responsibility of providing for his young family so late in life, and worry about what would happen to them after his death, pressed heavily upon him.

The superstitious parson experienced a run of bad luck during the last few years of his life, with accidents befalling those around him, storms causing structural damage on his farm, as well as cattle plague and potato blight. The portents were heavy, but he and his congregation had a lucky escape when part of the church roof collapsed during one of his services. The additional stress and strain of coping with all this led to him resorting to opium again.

Hawker and his wife made a trip to London to seek medical advice in 1874, and, after he had fallen ill during the harsh winter, the family took a springtime holiday with his brother Claud in Boscastle, hoping that the change of air would do him good. He longed to return home, but Pauline persuaded him to go to Plymouth to seek further medical advice. Just as they were about to return to his beloved Morwenstow, he suffered a stroke, and was converted to Roman Catholicism on his deathbed by Canon Mansfield, who had been summoned by his wife. Nobody could understand how this could be, and thus the man of contradictions remained an enigma to the end.

Although he had always wanted to be buried in the churchyard at Morwenstow, he was laid to rest in Plymouth cemetery, where his tomb bore the inscription 'I would not be forgotten in this land', taken from *The Quest of the Sangraal*. He will certainly never be forgotten in Cornwall, where his famous song *Trelawny* has become the unofficial anthem, and where his ghost is said to haunt the churchyard at Morwenstow.

8

Alfred Wallis 1855–1942

An Untutored Artistic Genius

The controversial St Ives painter Alfred Wallis might never have discovered his talent had he been able to claim an enormous family inheritance which seemingly should have come his way but was diverted elsewhere. In fact the tortured artist, who always had a dread of ending up in the workhouse and being buried in a pauper's grave, could have enjoyed a very different lifestyle, which might have prevented him from being featured as one of the heroic 'sons of Cornwall'.

Life had never been easy for the gifted man with family roots in West Penwith, whose grandfathers had both been seafarers. A few years after their marriage at Penzance Register Office in 1844, his parents moved to Devonport where their two surviving children, Charles and Alfred, were born. Employment opportunities associated with the construction of the breakwater in Plymouth Sound had probably prompted Charles senior and his wife Jane to move just across the Tamar, and the boys would have been familiar with the vibrant maritime scene all around them. Charles found work as a mason's labourer, before becoming a pavior, whose task it was to repair paving stones. The boys probably had a very rudimentary education, and Alfred remained semi-literate all his life.

Alfred, the younger of the two boys, was born on 8th August 1855, and throughout his life he mistakenly associated that day with the fall of 'Servesterpool', where he thought his father was at the time. Sebastapol actually fell a few weeks later. He used to give his date of birth as August 18th, but then, Alfred's account of his difficult life was full of conundrums. He claimed to have had 12 brothers and sisters, and that all but one were buried with his parents in Devonport cemetery, but this is not borne out by the official records. He also claimed in later life that he had run away to sea aged nine, working as a cabin boy and cook during his first trip across the Atlantic.

The two brothers were very close during their impoverished childhood, and were kept under strict control by their overbearing father, with his high moralistic values. Alfred developed into a shy and inhibited child who found it difficult to make friends and experienced terrible bouts of fear and loneliness. It was a cruel blow when his mother died, and the small and nimble, nervous little boy had to learn to fend for himself from a very tender age. The family returned to Penzance shortly afterwards. Charles Wallis senior found employment as a journeyman mason and his older son Charles became a labourer, while young Alfred was apprenticed to a basket-maker.

Penzance was a busy seaport at that time, and Alfred's brother Charles established himself as a marine store merchant, dealing in second-hand goods and renovating old fishing boats. He was also a rather pent up, inhibited and independent character, who did not relate easily to other people. He had become a hard drinking man, and he took up with Elizabeth Jane Williams, who had given birth to an illegitimate daughter in 1872, and who was also inclined to hit the bottle.

They got married in December 1876. Shortly after this, the two brothers, who had always been close and a comfort to each other, fell out over the matter of an inheritance. As with many episodes in Alfred's life, the story is somewhat obscure, with several variations, leading some commentators to use the phrase 'persecution mania'. It would seem that Charles, as the older brother, would have been in line for a fortune left by a deeply devout uncle who had struck it rich in mining in Australia. But Charles's name had been deleted from the will on account of his drinking habits, and Alfred thought that the money would come to him. But his brother apparently wrote to the executors of the will denying any knowledge of his younger brother's whereabouts and the money was subsequently bequeathed to a more distant relative.

Various records confirm that Alfred had become a mariner in the merchant service by the early 1870s. It was a very hard life, but the strong, nimble and diminutive young fellow was well able to handle the canvas and rigging of a light fore-and-aft schooner in a heavy North Atlantic gale, the feeling of which he was to convey so vividly in his paintings in later life.

As a young seafarer plying between Penzance and Newfoundland, Alfred had got to know George Ward, a smart young man four years his junior, who worked as a waiter at a Penzance hotel and drew Alfred into his family circle. George's father, Jacob, who had been a giant of a man, married petite Susan Ward in 1856, when she was 23 years old. Susan was skilled in the making of famous Honiton lace, and was a very capable woman who bore her husband many children. Her sought-after lace-making activities put her in touch with customers in the Penzance area, and the family moved to Madron to work for the land-owning Bolithos. The newcomers used to sing in the village choir at Madron Chapel, and the sight of the strapping six foot five husband out and about with his pint-sized wife caused some amusement in the village.

After the death of her husband, Susan and the children moved to New Street in Penzance, where she worked from dawn till dusk making lace, washing, scrubbing, ironing, baking and doing all she could to make ends meet. Alfred was made to feel welcome and got on well with George's energetic mother. He enjoyed being part of the cheerful rough and tumble of everyday family life, which had eluded him during his own stifled and curtailed childhood. Susan understood this, for she had been an orphan herself. Then dawned the day that the lodger, who had found a substitute mother, discovered that he was to become a father.

Alfred and Susan were married at St Mary's church in Penzance on 2nd April 1876, when he was 20 and she was 41. Thus the young bridegroom became stepfather to George, Albert, Emily, Jessie and Jacob, and the family's chief provider. This somewhat unorthodox set-up fulfilled some of Alfred's practical, physical and emotional needs at the time, and, as far as Susan was concerned, she had found security, companionship and an agreeable young bedfellow to liven up her middle age. The couple were teetotallers and God-fearing people, and Alfred's lugubrious look, accentuated by a droopy moustache, may have served to make the vast age difference less obvious. Be that as it may, Susan ruled the roost, and treated her spouse as one of the children.

Alfred was always generous towards his wife and stepchildren, and was looking forward to becoming a father himself. He continued his life as a seafarer on the Newfoundland run in the early days of his marriage, bringing in good money.

For centuries ships from Europe had traversed the notoriously stormy seas in quest of cod, which were abundant in the shallow waters off the coast of Newfoundland. The fish were caught, prepared and salted by fisherfolk living in obscure settlements along the indented coastline, to await collection by foreign vessels. The much sought-after dried and salted product was invaluable for ships on long voyages, and provided nutritious provender for warring armies.

At that time a number of small West Country sailing schooners, known as 'cod bankers', were plying this traditional route, with the manoeuvrability to cope with tight situations along rugged coastlines. These flat sheered Cornish schooners, which were very wide across the fore-rigging where the beam was at its greatest and tapered aft, were described by local seafarers as having a 'gurnet's head and a mackerel's tail'. They were usually deep, required a lot of ballast and could mount a sea with ease.

These fast and beautiful ships were apparently designed for speed and sailing qualities rather than commercial viability. Some of the rugged old timers worshipped their vessels and treated them as living beings. The grace and dignity of such sailing ships, the taut ropes, the swelling canvas and the billowing waves made a tremendous impact on young Alfred, which was to find colourful and lively expression many years later. He spent several happy years at sea, before becoming involved with the local fishing scene around Penzance and Newlyn, after a tragedy which affected him deeply.

The story according to Alfred was that he and his shipmates got to know the crew of another schooner while docked at St John's, Newfoundland, waiting to return home to England. The other schooner left the day before Alfred's ship was due to depart and the two crews wished each other God speed and looked forward to meeting up in England. But it was not to be as the other schooner got caught up in a heavy gale and the ship was lost with all hands. Unaware of this at the time, Alfred's skipper set sail the following day and also encountered foul weather in the mid-Atlantic.

It proved to be a gruelling test of seamanship and endurance, and they owed their survival to their ability to form a human chain and pass the cargo up from the hold before jettisoning it overboard. This allowed the vessel to right herself but during the operation they were driven a long way off course, which delayed their homecoming. Meanwhile Susan was waiting anxiously at home and when she received news that his ship had been lost, she gave birth prematurely, and Alfred's son died a few months later. Alfred subsequently gave up deep sea voyages in favour of local fishing, supplemented by labouring work ashore. Sadly a daughter, Ellen Jane, born on 25th May 1879, also died in infancy. Both children were buried in unmarked graves in Madron cemetery.

Although Alfred was deprived of the joy of having his own

children, he became a substitute grandfather after Susan's children married and moved away. It eased some of his loneliness and was some repayment for all the hard work he had put in to bringing up his ready-made family. It was a bitter blow to him when in later life he discovered that Susan had continued to help her children out financially, even when they were leading their own lives, eroding the savings Alfred had expected to be put aside to keep them in old age.

Alfred moved his family to St Ives in the early 1880s and established himself as a marine stores dealer. He bought up scrap iron, sails, rope and other paraphernalia and would tour the town with a sack on his back, crying out 'Rag-a-bone! Old iron! Rag-a-bone!', which earnt him the nickname of 'Old Iron'. He would then sell this on to a scruffy character called Denley, from Penzance, who was said to be worth a fortune when he died.

Alfred operated from premises in Back Road before moving up Bethesda Hill and then to the Wharf. As his business grew he got himself a donkey called Neddy and a spring cart. He created a stable in his cellar with a door, enabling Neddy to see what was going on in the street. He was fond of the donkey, and was very upset when it died.

It was a family business. Jacob's mother-in-law used to help out with the book-keeping, while Susan would sort out the pile of junk in the cellar ready for Denley's man to collect once a fortnight with two wagons. Alfred would accompany him to Penzance with his spring-cart, and always felt elated on the journey home, admiring the noble granite landscape with commanding views of the mighty Atlantic and recalling happy times on the old windjammers. Alfred would have seen many of the sophisticated artists of the established St Ives colony, painting at their easels out on the waterfront, and could never have imagined at that time that he would emerge as the most notable, if controversial, of the lot, with his work destined to be displayed with pride in the prestigious Tate St Ives art gallery.

Susan had always been the dominant partner in the marriage, with a firm hold on the purse strings. She had become an ardent Salvationist before leaving Penzance, and held religious meetings in the fishermen's cottages as well as being a Sunday school teacher. Alfred eventually saw the light and became a member of the Salvation Army in 1904, although he wanted to be free to interpret the Bible in his own way. Being so much older than her husband, Susan had been thinking about their needs in old age and retirement, and in 1908, when she was 75 and he was 57, Alfred purchased no. 3 Back Road for £93. He continued with his rag-and-bone trade, which was dependent on the viability of the harbour and the local fishing industry. But, in the years leading up to the outbreak of the First World War, the large stern trawlers from East Anglia were having a detrimental effect on the Cornish fisheries and this led to a decline in Alfred 's business.

Wallis, Alfred, Marine Stores Dealer closed for business in

The waterfront site of 'Wallis, Alfred, Marine Stores Dealer'. (Sheila Bird collection)

1912. Alfred went around doing odd jobs and found himself working for Mr Armour, an antiques dealer, providing some insight into the world of objets d'art.

The couple lived a quiet domestic life in their basic little home in Back Road. Their front door opened directly into the living room, with a screened off scullery beyond and an indoor earth closet. A small wooden staircase led to the bedroom above. They cooked on a Cornish range and had simple furnishings, with family photographs adorning the walls. In her declining years Susan worked at her bobbins by the fireside, enjoying the companionship of her husband, and reading the Good Book with him. After the closure of his business Alfred became increasingly withdrawn from society, and people regarded him as a bit strange in the head and unpredictable. It was a tremendous blow to him when Susan, his only companion, died in 1922.

The hard working widower had been experiencing financial difficulties since the closing down of his marine stores, and in 1915 he was summoned to appear at the town hall for failure to pay the poor rate. At this time of heartache and loneliness he made the dreadful discovery that the money he and Susan had put by amongst their best bed linen and blankets in a trunk in the bedroom had vanished, and the bedding had been replaced by worn-out stuff. Various members of the family had paid Susan frequent visits when she was ill, but Albert Ward was thought to be the culprit, because he had been dealing with their laundry every week. Alfred also thought that he had amassed a substantial amount of money for his old age, but Susan had been dipping into his savings for her children over the years. He became embittered, saying that he wished he had never met the Ward family. He was so short of money that he sold his cottage on the understanding that he could remain in it for the rest of his life, at a nominal rent.

Having now alienated himself from almost everybody, the unhappy man tried to fend for himself as best he could, living in poverty and inhibited by his complexes and eccentricities. He was fearful of the evil spirits, whose voices he fancied he heard coming down the chimney. He read from the Bible every day, and, if he was lucky enough to have company, would point to it saying that everything a man needed to know was written there. Sometimes he played a tune or two on his old Salvation Army accordion. Then, one day, he took up a brush and started to create images of those much loved sailing vessels from his past on some old piece of junk, using ordinary household paint. This had a calming, therapeutic effect on him and he started painting more and more, giving away the end results to local people, who sometimes sniggered over them and threw them in the bin.

The septuagenarian budding artist became very prolific between his panic attacks. He painted on odd pieces of paper and cardboard, advertising cards and discarded calendars, with brushes purchased from a local hardware shop. He did not trim the irregular shapes, in fact he sometimes accentuated them with his scissors, making this the keynote of an original composition in his highly individual style. Unlike the professional painters who set up their easels in the open air in fine weather, Alfred painted indoors, from memory and imagination, with his recycled materials on a flat table by the front door.

On the face of it his paintings had a vibrant, simple, childlike quality, rather than being visually correct in regard to perspective and proportions. This spontaneous freedom allowed him to create his own engaging order of things, particularly in his maritime paintings. His was a literal style, depicting what was there. It was almost as if he were observing the scene from several different angles at once, thus conveying greater feeling and a deeper insight than would have been possible with tutored correctness. This delightful piece of personal poetic licence probably occurred because he was working on a flat surface, and walking around the four sides of a table, rather than sitting at an easel in the conventional way. Thus any perspective there may be

A charming portrayal of trawlers by Alfred Wallis. (Private collection)

tends to be an aerial one. Many of his maritime paintings have a main focal object, while those depicting places possess a map-like quality. Alfred must always have been observant and had great recall, for some of the street scenes are reminiscent of his childhood haunts, and ports he may have visited as a seaman, as well as depicting St Ives.

The locals regarded Alfred as an eccentric curiosity, and were dismissive of his talents. Sven Berlin, who published a book about him in 1949, said that the 'members of the St Ives Society, with their academic distinctions, their hidebound unprogressive attitude to painting, when they noticed him at all, considered him quite unimportant, and smiled at his work like condescending giraffes.'

The modest and unassuming, intuitive painter was first discovered by established artists Ben Nicholson and Christopher

Wood in August 1928, who on a day trip to St Ives had noticed some of his depictions of ships and houses on odd scraps of paper and cardboard nailed to his walls as they paused by his open front door. They were enchanted by his work and bought some paintings, which were much admired by influential figures in the art world of the day. These included H.S. Ede, Herbert Read, Adrian Stokes, Geoffrey Grigson, John Aldridge, Helen Sutherland, Barbara Hepworth and many others. Ede took a particular interest in Alfred and did much to promote his work. He had several paintings hanging in his office at the Tate Gallery. They hailed him as an untutored artistic genius of the 'primitive' style.

Although outwardly dour and undemonstrative, Alfred was tickled pink to find that his paintings were being appreciated and taken seriously, and, although he appeared indifferent about the money received, was very proud about selling his work. He used to parcel up paintings in old brown paper held together with lengths of knotted string, which were eagerly awaited by his widening circle of admirers.

He used to say that he was not a real painter (like those in the art colony around him), and that he did it 'for company'. During his lifetime Alfred's paintings found their way into galleries in London, New York and other places, as well as many private collections, and were reproduced in many books on art. But he was unworldly and always flattered that anyone would want to buy his paintings, however small the sum. This naivety was exploited and the artist himself benefited very little from the sale of his paintings; and it did not ameliorate his pressing circumstances.

Alfred enjoyed talking about his paintings, and could be good company and fun to be with at times. Sven Berlin recognised that his phobias and complexes were an integral part of his creativity, and that his repressed feelings were expressed in the violence of some of his paintings. Furthermore, he perceived sexual imagery, phallic symbols, celestial female symbols and eroticism in some of Alfred's pictures, and wondered whether he would have produced such lively paintings if he had had a happier and more fulfilled life. Sven Berlin cited Alfred as 'the Primitive' of the 20th century, declaring that 'only an unassuming and rugged nature could have produced such work in an age of so much barren, self-conscious, intellectual snobbery and power.'

The outbreak of the Second World War had a very disruptive effect on the fates and fortunes of those in the rarefied world of art. By that time Alfred, now in his mid 80s, was becoming increasingly frail and troubled by occasional bouts of mental illness. His nephew William Wallis and a few good friends did what they could to help, and, although he declared that he never wanted to leave his own fireside, and had always had a dread of ending up in the workhouse, it got to the point that he felt unable to cope any longer and resigned himself to being carted off to the workhouse in Madron, taking only his watch, his magnifying glass and scissors, in June 1941. His prestigious artist friends had discussed ways of saving him from such a fate from time to time, but never actually got around to doing anything about it.

Alfred had been suffering from bronchitis at the time of his arrival at the workhouse, and he was confined to bed for about a month. A number of people of some standing visited him there, impressing on its Master in a diplomatic way that Alfred was an important person; in fact 'one of the best painters in England'. This improved his standing with the staff and fellow inmates, and as he settled down he adapted himself quite well to being part of a small community, albeit in very drab and austere surroundings. He had declared that he would never paint again when he left for the workhouse, but he asked his artist friends to fetch his painting materials from his cottage, and produced a number of paintings and drawings, mainly in pencil and greasy crayon. Apparently he achieved some startling results in a variety of styles reminiscent of Greek draughtsmanship, Picasso, Van

Gogh, and Chinese and Japanese artists, despite his failing eyesight and a host of other physical and psychiatric problems.

The former marine scrap metal dealer who found freedom from the stresses and strains of life through his art, and thus an enduring place in history, died in August 1942. Although he had ended up in the workhouse, he was spared the humiliation of being buried in a pauper's grave, thanks to an artist friend who bridged the gap with his savings and arranged a decent funeral, which was carried out by the Salvation Army. His headstone in the churchyard above Porthmeor Beach features a golden lighthouse in large pottery tiles, designed by the famous potter Bernard Leach. It is a stone's throw from the prestigious Tate Gallery, where his much sought after paintings are exhibited with pride. His work has influenced many others, and he has been much copied.

Fate had played many tricks on this complex Cornish hero, who found fame but not fortune. If he had inherited the money he thought was due to him and become a rich man, would he have bothered to paint? Would he have had professional training? If he had been tutored would he have lost his unique brand of magic? Perhaps the most poignant tribute to this modest, unassuming man came from Mr and Mrs Gabo at the time of his funeral. It read, 'In homage to the artist on whom Nature has bestowed the rarest of gifts, not to know that he is one.'

9

The Heroes of Mount's Bay

A Special Breed of Men

They were truly the bravest eight men I've ever seen who were also totally dedicated to upholding the highest standards of the RNLI.

(Lt Cdr Russell L. Smith, USN Pilot of RN Sea King helicopter 'Rescue 80', December 1981)

The deeds performed by SAR (Search & Rescue) flyers often demand quite extraordinary degrees of heroism and stamina. Like lifeboatmen, they are a special breed, driven by a flinty sense of duty, a readiness to serve others and a refreshing tendency to cut the cackle and get on with the job in hand.

(John Beattie: *Drama in the Air*)

The south coast of Cornwall, with its proudly jutting headlands, spectacular rocky bays and fine river estuaries, which look so benign and beautiful in the tourist brochures, has also been the scene of countless shipwrecks throughout the ages. In the days of sail the fate of sailors and their ships was all too often revealed along the coastline in the cold, clear light of a cruel Cornish dawn. The area around Land's End, which has double tides, complex currents and vulnerability to the full fury of Atlantic storms, has always been notorious with seafarers the world over. The curve of Mount's Bay might offer protection to shipping in some conditions, but a sudden swing in wind direction could turn this apparently safe haven into a death trap.

The on-going catalogue of disasters in Mount's Bay with appalling loss of life led to a special appeal fund being set up, which resulted in the first lifeboat in Cornwall being placed at Penzance in 1803. Furthermore there was the distinction of local men William Rowe and John Freeman being awarded early Silver Medals of the future RNLI in 1824, for saving the crew of the collier brig called *Olive*, wrecked beneath the Halzephron cliffs on the eastern side of the bay.

This lifeboat station, which came to be sited at Newlyn and Penlee, lies near the head of the majestic bay, which sweeps round from Gwennap Head, near Land's End to Lizard Point. In 1859, a lifeboat station was established at Polpeor Cove on this awesome, rocky eastern extremity of Mount's Bay, where so many vessels were driven on-shore by the ferocious south-westerlies. A lifeboat station had been established at Sennen Cove, just north of Land's End, to cope with emergencies around that notorious section of seaway in 1853. As lifeboats developed the capacity to cover a wider area, the stations at Porthleven and Mullion on the eastern shores of Mount's Bay were closed, and St Mary's lifeboat from the Isles of Scilly provided back up for the Land's End patch when necessary.

Before the establishment of lifeboat stations, rescues had been carried out by fishermen in their own boats, and it was customary for the local seafaring fraternity to keep watch from the shore, particularly in time of impending storm. The Coastguard service was initially set up to stamp out smuggling but evolved to meet a variety of changing situations. A branch of this service, known as the Preventive Water Guard, operating inshore, was the forerunner of HM Coastguard. Coastguard instructions of 1829 were concerned with discipline, good relations with kindred organisations and their responsibilities in regard to the prevention of smuggling and shipwreck, when the onus was on them to preserve life, take charge of the vessel and protect property.

In 1831, the service was seen by the Admiralty as a convenient means of manning the fleet in times of war. Naval style uniforms were introduced, and as reservists the men were obliged to undergo naval training, thereby acquiring a host of invaluable skills in regard to handling emergency situations by land and sea. While under the control of the Admiralty they had collected an astonishing range of responsibilities towards various organisations, including the RNLI, Trinity House, the Fisheries, the Air Ministry, the Home Office, the Post Office, and Lloyds, as well as weather forecasting. The Coastguard service could also proudly lay claim to being at the forefront of conservation, in that it established an early responsibility towards the Royal Society for the Protection of Wild Birds.

When the Board of Trade assumed responsibility for the Coastguards on April 1st 1923, they retained the title His Majesty's Coastguard by royal sanction. Thus, they became a professional life saving force, keeping watch around our coasts and working in conjunction with the RNLI and other life saving services. The RNLI has retained its status as a charity, whereas the Coastguards are under the control of a government department.

Technology moved on apace after the Second World War, and this was reflected in improved communications and the design of lifeboats. In early times, when the only way ships in distress could communicate with the shore was by visual means, watch was kept from lookouts spaced along our coastline. But the development of radio (initially Morse code signals transmitted by telegraph), telephone and increasing use of VHF improved communications immeasurably. This led to vast changes in the Coastguard service, which invested its resources in radio watch. Nevertheless, the local seafaring fraternity still knows the value of constant vigilance from the cliff tops and an intimate knowledge of the area.

In 1978 the Coastguard service was reorganised for operations to be centralised from Maritime Rescue Co-ordination Centres (MRCCs), such as that at Pendennis Point, Falmouth, opened by

HRH Prince Charles, the Honorary Commodore of HM Coastguard, on 2nd December 1981. This was the nerve centre for Maritime Search and Rescue for the coastal area from Dodman Point to the Isles of Scilly, and northwards to a point near Hartland, and extending halfway across the Atlantic. Falmouth also had the distinction of being the sole UK terminal for INMARSAT maritime satellite distress communications via the British Telecom Earth Receiving Station at Goonhilly, on the Lizard Peninsula.

The first lifeboat to arrive in Penzance, back in 1803, had been built by Henry Greathead of South Shields, but there was a reluctance to use it as the local seafarers had greater faith in their own craft, which they knew were built to suit the conditions around their home shores. The early lifeboats were pulling and sailing craft of varying lengths, open to the elements with the oarsmen wearing air belts and later cork lifejackets to keep them afloat in an emergency. The skill and endurance of those pioneer lifeboatmen is almost beyond belief, and their heroism was recognised on many occasions.

Getting a lifeboat launched through the surf was always a hazardous business, and this and other problems led to the lifeboat being sited at various points around the waterfront at Penzance, Wherrytown, Newlyn and Penlee, situated halfway between Newlyn and Mousehole. The Penlee station, which opened in 1913, had a slipway providing an efficient, fast afloat launching, close to Land's End. The first lifeboat to be stationed there was the heavy, 12-oared Watson class *Elizabeth and Blanche*, which had also seen service at Penzance and Newlyn. Alterations and enlargements were made when *The Brothers*, the first of three motor Watson class lifeboats, arrived in 1922.

The service record of the *Elizabeth and Blanche* had demonstrated the shift in emphasis from sailing vessels in distress to steamships, which required more speed and power in rescue craft. The new motor lifeboat soon proved her worth, and, while it was clear that such lifeboats could ease the punishing physical demands of their predecessors, the increased capabilities gave rise to a greater range of hazards in this area near the toe of Cornwall, which had long justified its reputation as a 'maritime trap' amongst seafarers.

The second motor lifeboat, the *W&S*, short for Winifred Alice Coode and Sidney Webb, which arrived in August 1931, was regarded with great affection among the local lifeboat fraternity, because of the many brave rescues carried out. In particular there was the service to the SS *Taycraig* on 27th January 1936, which had struck Gear Rock during a strong south-south-westerly gale. When the lifeboat arrived on the scene at 02.45 that night the casualty was lying end-on to the gale, offering no lee for shelter. Despite the *W&S* being hurled violently about and narrowly missing being flung on the vessel's deck, the coxswain managed to get her alongside, allowing the crew to make a jump for safety and even retrieving one crew member who landed in the sea. This bold, slick service, which saved nine lives, earned the station's longest serving coxswain, Frank Blewett, a Bronze Medal.

Then there were the dramatic events surrounding the mission to HMS *Warspite* in April 1947, which became legendary. It was Edwin Madron's first service as coxswain.

The defiant old battleship *Warspite* was undergoing the indignity of being towed to a scrap yard on the Clyde in a strengthening south-westerly gale, when she broke adrift and went aground on Mount Malpas Ledge near Cudden Point. The *W&S* launched through the heavy seas, and managed to get within hailing distance to warn the skeleton crew of their predicament in a worsening situation on a rising tide, and advise them to abandon ship. The Master declined to do so, regarding it as impossible to get aboard the lifeboat in such wild conditions. The weather deteriorated and the *W&S*, which had diverted to Newlyn, set out a second time, and discovered the casualty in a more vulnerable situation, ashore to the east of Prussia Cove, in close proximity to rocks with heavy seas breaking around them. Coxswain Edwin Madron, pumping oil on the angry waters, heroically took the lifeboat into a narrow channel between the ship and the rocks, where there was a rise and fall of 30 feet, and got two lines aboard. Then, with great skill and clever timing, the lifeboat was manoeuvred backwards and forwards in anticipation of the movement of the waves, allowing each of the eight men to leap aboard; a process which took 35 minutes.

For this magnificent St George's Day rescue, Coxswain Madron received the RNLI's Silver Medal, the mechanic John Drew the Bronze Medal and the crew the Institution's Thanks on Vellum. The coxswain also received the Maud Smith Award for the bravest lifeboat deed that year. The *W&S* continued her fine record of service, mostly with fishing vessels, motor vessels and steamships, until being replaced by the splendid new Watson type lifeboat *Solomon Browne* in September 1960.

The *Solomon Browne*, which was basically of traditional design, but with an enclosed cockpit, was constructed by William Osborne of Littlehampton, and fitted out with the latest equipment. She was 47 feet long, had a beam of 13 feet, a draught of five feet and twin screws driven by two 60hp diesel engines. There were tunnels to protect the propellers, the engine room had a double bottom and her hull was divided into six watertight compartments, fitted with 216 air cases. During her particularly fine record of 21 years of service she was launched scores of times and underwent several overhauls. Her crew recalled incidents, such as the 36 hour standby during the *Torrey Canyon* disaster of 1967, when they returned exhausted, and faced the daunting task of removing all trace of oil from her before returning home.

The Second Coxswain, Mechanic Stephen Madron, Edwin's grandson, explained to me, during an interview in July 1981, that 'standby' was more wearing than getting to grips with the task in hand. He remembered the Fastnet Race of August 1979,

The Watson class lifeboat Solomon Browne, which came on station in 1960, was lost with her entire crew while going to the aid of the coaster Union Star in December 1981. (Courtesy RNLI, photograph by H.G. Welby)

mostly for the frustration of being on standby for 48 hours. 'We were ordered to wait in case another emergency arose. Care has to be taken that lifeboats are available when help may urgently be needed. Eventually we were called out to tow one of the yachts back.' He went on to make the comment that the lifeboatmen of old in their sailing and rowing open boats were real heroes, whereas modern lifeboatmen had it easy.

During her time on station, the *Solomon Browne* was particularly associated with 'medico' services, bringing sick seamen ashore or taking doctors out to ships. Like other RNLI craft she was experiencing an increasing number of callouts to holidaymakers with little or no experience of the sea. I asked Stephen whether he considered some people irresponsible in the way they did silly things, putting their own lives and the lives of others in danger.

'We're here to provide assistance; not to make judgements,' he replied. 'Anyone who feels like that should not be in the lifeboat service. There is no training for ordinary people to put to sea. If they get into difficulties, it is because they don't know what they are doing. It's ignorance, not deliberate. I never met anyone who deliberately got into difficulties, even the experts sometimes make mistakes.' He illustrated this last point with the story of an experienced crew of a famous sailing ship which started sinking off Land's End because the pumps had been blocked with shavings after the last refit.

Stephen said his most memorable service was that of the MV *Lovat* in January 1975, probably on account of the personal and emotional aspect. Shortly after returning from Swansea, where he had been working for Trinity House, the maroons sounded, and as everyone went flying about he heard the ship's name being mentioned, but could not quite place it at first. Then it transpired that the vessel had just left Swansea, and he was to find himself hauling lifeless bodies aboard, and looking into the faces of drinking associates of a few days before. 'Dealing with dead bodies is a gruesome task which has to be done. Recognising some of the faces of people you were chatting to and drinking with just a short time ago, really brings it home to you.' For this service carried out in appalling weather conditions, Coxswain Trevelyan Richards received the Institution's Bronze Medal, and his crew Thanks on Vellum.

The weather had been unseasonably fine on Friday, 18th December, but a gale suddenly erupted the following day, rising to hurricane force by the evening. The wind, blowing from south by east, increased to force 12, gusting to 90 knots, producing mountainous seas, later described by a highly experienced mariner as the worst he had ever seen in regard to the size and steepness of the waves, which rose to a height of about 60 feet as they neared the shore.

At 18.04 on Saturday, December 19th the recently opened

Falmouth Coastguard Station intercepted a call from the *Union Star*, a new 1,400 ton coaster on passage from Holland to Southern Ireland. She reported engine failure an estimated eight miles east of Wolf Rock Lighthouse and had eight people on board. This included Captain Moreton's wife and two stepdaughters, who were unofficial passengers. He had alerted the Coastguard to request a tow and provision for his family to be taken off should they be unable to restart the engines.

It was the captain's responsibility to determine the level of assistance he required. The Coastguard alerted the various rescue services. RNAS (Royal Naval Air Station) Culdrose and the Penlee Lifeboat were informed, and a Sea King helicopter was placed in a state of readiness. The offer of a tow from the Dutch tug *Noord Holland*, which was in the vicinity, was turned down by Captain Moreton, who was reluctant to involve the ship's owners in a costly salvage deal unless it was absolutely essential. He had high hopes of getting the engines restarted. The Dutch captain was very concerned about the vessel's plight in rapidly worsening sea conditions, and set in motion communications between his company and the *Union Star's* owners in Kent. Throughout this epic drama there were problems in contacting the relevant authorities on a Saturday night in the run-up to Christmas, and a desire to observe protocol, resulting in an unfortunate series of delays. At 19.20 Captain Moreton agreed to the Coastguard broadcasting Pan Pan, signifying that help was needed urgently, but there was no immediate danger. He had been authorised by Union Transport plc of Kent, to accept assistance from the tug *Noord Holland*, which was now proceeding to the area. The radar at Land's End Coastguard Station gave indications that the vessel was drifting towards the shore.

A Sea King helicopter (Rescue 80) left Culdrose at 19.37, having been requested to take off a woman and two children on this wild winter's night, with a wind speed of over 60 knots gusting to 80. The sea beneath them was very disturbed with 40 ft waves, and they were surprised to encounter sea spray as they dropped to 400 ft. When they sighted the coaster's red flare, she was only two miles from Tater Du. The vessel's close proximity to this notoriously high, rocky and unyielding coastline led the Falmouth Coastguard to request the Penlee Lifeboat to launch immediately, and to ask for a co-ordinated response from the cliff rescue services. Coastguard Sector Officer Don Buckfield, who had been manning the radar screen at Land's End, was directed to take charge of operations from Mousehole.

As the lifeboatmen converged on the old boathouse on the cliffs at Penlee in worsening storm conditions on this dark, horrendous night, coxswain Trevelyan Richards picked his brave crew of seven. He turned away 17 year old Neil Brockman, who arrived with his father Nigel, saying, 'One from each family is enough on a night like this.' They were exposed to the full force of the elements as soon as the boathouse doors were opened, and the lifeboat was launched down the slipway into those angry seas. Getting the lifeboat launched in such difficult conditions was a stern test of courage and seamanship in itself, for no one could remember anything like it.

The helicopter crew also had their skills put to the test endeavouring to hover in those strong, gusting winds above the *Union Star*, which was wallowing and rolling, with the heavy seas cascading over her decks. They were working with the aid of spotlights. The design of the coaster with its superstructure aft, a variety of obstacles on the decks and a swaying radar aerial attached to the 50 ft mast, presented a challenge for airborne rescue. The unpredictable motion of the mast was a hazard for a winchman attempting to land on the deck, and could foul the helicopter's rotors with devastating consequences. Furthermore the design of the rather bulky Sea King, restricting the pilot's view in regard to landing a winchman, required the use of internally transmitted instructions. There was no room for error, and faith and trust were essential for pilot Lt Commander Russell Smith of the US Navy, his co-pilot, observer, who was also the winch operator, and the winchman.

Captain Moreton remained adamant that only his wife and two stepdaughters were to be taken off at this stage. The heroic helicopter crew made repeated attempts to lift them off, with the helicopter being buffeted around, and winchman Steven Marlow being swung this way and that through the air above the rising and falling vessel. They almost made it several times, but were forced to stand off and reassess the situation after the reeling mast narrowly missed the winchman and the main rotors. In fact a crewman had actually caught hold of the line on one occasion, but had been forced to let it go, although no attempt was made to take it when it landed close by on another occasion.

The captain thought that his ship could be saved when they managed to restart one of the generators, even though his re-activated radar was now able to demonstrate their close proximity to the shore. He thanked the helicopter crew for their assistance and said he was going to put an anchor down. This left them bow-on to the sea, but drifting more slowly towards the shore. When the *Noord Holland* came on the scene Captain Buurman knew that the casualty was too close to the shallow, rocky shore to allow them to carry out the necessary manoeuvres to fix a tow.

The tug and helicopter remained close by when the Penlee lifeboat arrived on the scene, having taken a battering and having been swamped and in danger of capsizing on her two and a half mile passage from the boathouse. As soon as they rounded Tater Du they became fully aware of the coaster's perilous situation. She was being driven into a small shallow bay full of rocks and shoals, and they knew they would have no protection from the lee for a rescue attempt in such atrocious conditions. They offered to go alongside to take off the woman and her two daughters but the helicopter crew, who had been having problems in trying to create a longer, heavier line, decided to make a final attempt with a weighted bag to hold it down, but this got washed away by an exceptionally powerful wave.

Everything now depended on the coxswain and the crew of the *Solomon Browne*, who would brave every danger in the long established idealistic aim of seafarers to 'preserve life from shipwreck'. By now the winds had risen to hurricane force 12, with the waves reaching a height of 50 to 60 feet, as witnessed by the helicopter crew and Captain Buurman, who had never experienced anything like it in all his years at sea.

At 20.57 the coxswain made radio contact with the stricken vessel informing them of his intention to come in close on the port side. After the captain's lengthy procrastinations it was now agreed that they should all leave the ship. The waves became higher and steeper and more chaotic as they reached the shallows, and the force of the rain-lashed wind was enough to stun and knock anyone off their feet. At this time the coxswain, engineer and radio operator were at the controls, while the other five lifeboatmen positioned themselves on the heaving deck with their lifelines clipped on and heavy grappling ropes at the ready. They fired white flares to illuminate the scene, and were also assisted by lights from the helicopter. As the *Solomon Browne* closed in for the first time with her bow facing seaward to allow for a swift getaway, the two vessels were thrown against each other with considerable force. The lifeboatmen took this opportunity to get the lines over the ship's rails and urge the people up on the bridge to make a dash for it. However, they had to take swift action to avoid capsizing when a mountainous wave suddenly reared up out of the darkness.

The lifeboat made repeated attempts to get alongside the *Union Star*, which was getting closer inshore and bucking, rearing and rolling as mighty waves met her bow-on. After each attempt the *Solomon Browne* went around and was deftly manoeuvred back alongside. During the course of this she was repeatedly thrown against the ship's side, but her sturdy construction withstood these batterings. There were several occasions when the stranded victims could have got aboard, and the helicopter winchman,

Steve Marlow, was later to state, 'The over-riding thought I have is the reluctance of the victims to be rescued – their reluctance to come out on the decks to both ourselves and the lifeboat.'

At 21.05 the helicopter pilot warned of their closeness to the shore. With winds gusting up to 100 mph and very poor visibility, the helicopter was also getting into an increasingly tight situation, with the danger of the tail rotor striking the cliffs. Meanwhile the Coastguards, who had been directed to Lamorna by Falmouth MRCC, were battling their way south-westwards over steep and rough terrain in dark and difficult conditions. When they reached Carn Barges they spotted the lights of the *Noord Holland* out at sea, then they were appalled to catch sight of the lifeboat making manoeuvres in such a vulnerable situation just the other side of Tater Du. Thereupon they headed for Tater Du and summoned back-up from the Sennen and St Levan rescue teams.

The lifeboatmen's valiant efforts to save those in peril prompted the helicopter crew to have another go, albeit in conditions worse than before. In fact the winchman made two attempts, and had a very near miss himself when a projecting sponson probably saved him from being struck by the rotor. By this time the *Union Star* had turned broadside in the breakers, thus providing a better opportunity to get people off. Those in the helicopter saw the lifeboat make another run-in, but as she did so she was caught by a huge wave, which lifted her onto the casualty's hatch covers. The larger vessel gave a lurch and she promptly slid stern first back into the water, remaining afloat and under control. Then, to the amazement of those watching, she made another swift and skilful manoeuvre back alongside, picked up some survivors and got herself clear of the dangerous breakers. At 21.21 the Penlee lifeboat sent a message to Falmouth Coastguard stating that they had got four people off, but two remained aboard the casualty. (The other two, who had probably been swept overboard by this time, would not have survived for long in such dreadful conditions.)

The last message from the *Solomon Browne* had ended abruptly, but the helicopter crew had seen her heading out to sea, and returned to Culdrose. Captain Buurman saw her high on the crest of a wave, backlit by the coaster's lights, which were extinguished as she was struck by a huge wall of water and thrown onto the rocks at the foot of the cliff, landing keel uppermost.

Those arriving in the vicinity overland suddenly became aware of the pungent smell of diesel, and when they reached the cliff edge they beheld the shocking sight of the upturned casualty with waves breaking across her. Two of them thought they saw a figure leap from the wheelhouse into the raging waters, whereupon brave Don Buckfield instructed his men to lower him over the edge of the cliff to investigate. He found the shore littered with debris from the storm and discovered more wreckage when he descended a deep gully at the head of the constricted shallow bay. But there was no sign of any survivors. (He was subsequently awarded a Silver Medal of the Royal Humane Society for his on-going actions in regard to this catastrophic night.)

The Falmouth Coastguard, the Dutch tug, R80's crew and associates back in Newlyn made repeated attempts to contact the Penlee Lifeboat, but could get no response. The authorities and local folk were becoming increasingly anxious, but there was great relief when they heard reports of lights being spotted, which were taken to be those of the returning lifeboat. The media started to relay the optimistic news, and continued to do so long after the painful realisation that it had aroused false hopes. In the darkness, as the storm raged on, Coastguard rescue teams carried out the dangerous task of combing the coastline, while the helicopter re-appeared on the scene to carry out a search and rescue operation for the lifeboat and their colleagues who had been so courageous in their selfless endeavours to save the lives of others.

It had now become a situation with Mayday! being broadcast in regard to the 'overdue' Penlee Lifeboat. The neighbouring lifeboats at the Sennen and Lizard/Cadgwith RNLI stations were called out to assist in these hurricane-torn waters, as well as the newly acquired 52 ft Arun class *Robert Edgar* from St Mary's in the Isles of Scilly. The Sennen lifeboat encountered impossible conditions as she attempted to round Land's End, and had to turn back. St Mary's splendid new lifeboat, coxswained by Matt Lethbridge, sped through the hazardous waters to reach the search area, where she was joined by the Lizard/Cadgwith lifeboat, which had had a very punishing time getting there. Shortly after her arrival three crewmen narrowly escaped being washed overboard by a mountainous wave. Meanwhile a nightmare scenario had developed at Lamorna Cove, where pieces of wreckage had been identified as coming from the *Solomon Browne*. Some of the victims' bodies from the *Solomon Browne* and the *Union Star* were subsequently recovered, and the stern section of the lifeboat was towed from St Michael's Mount to Newlyn by Matt Lethbridge and his crew, who had worked tirelessly for hours on end. A rope was found to be entangled around her propeller.

The entire crew of the Penlee lifeboat had been lost in this disaster, together with the eight people who had been aboard the *Union Star*. For their gallantry, the RNLI posthumously awarded a Gold Medal to Coxswain William Trevelyan Richards, and Bronze Medals to Second Coxswain Mechanic James Stephen Madron, Assistant Mechanic Nigel Brockman, Emergency Mechanic John Robert Blewett, and Crew Members Charles Thomas Greenhaugh, Kevin Smith, Barrie Robertson Torrie and Gary Lee Wallis.

News pictures flashed across the world and touched the hearts of people everywhere. This harrowing event did more than anything else in recent times to bring the selfless devotion of lifeboat men and the role of the RNLI to the attention of the general public. Locally, people were shocked and grief stricken; the proud little fishing community of Mousehole, which had lost so many brave men in one cruel night, was stunned. But thoughts were quickly focused on the overwhelming prospect of forming an instant

Stephen Madron, Mechanic, and the lifeboat Solomon Browne *at the boathouse at Penlee Point, 31st July 1981. (Sheila Bird)*

replacement crew. In normal circumstances men would be absorbed into the crew one at a time, to maintain continuity; coxswains would emerge naturally, with a close knowledge of the station and its crew. An instant coxswain in the wake of lost heroes would have been a difficult role to play.

The Penlee lifeboat, which has been stationed afloat in Newlyn Harbour since that time, has subsequently carried out many fine services, including one to the *Julian Paul* in December 1994, for which they and the Sennen Cove station were awarded Bronze Medals. In October 1992, Neil Brockman, who had been turned away by Trevelyan Richards on that ill-fated mission eleven years earlier, but lost his father in the tragedy, was proud to don his coxswain's hat for the very first time.

Penlee's Severn class lifeboat Ivan Ellen *lies in readiness alongside the pontoon in Newlyn Harbour. (Sheila Bird)*

'Been out in the lifeboat often?'
'Aye, aye, Sir, often enough.'
'When it's rougher than this?'
'Why bless you this ain't what we calls rough!
It's when there's a gale a blowing,
And the white seas roll in and break
On the shore, with a roar like thunder,
And the tall cliffs seem to shake,
When the sea is a hell of waters,
And the bravest holds his breath,
As he hears the cry for the lifeboat
His summons may be to his death.
That's when we call it rough, Sir,
But if we can get her afloat
There's always enough brave fellows
Ready to man the boat.'
(By Dagonet – alias George Robert Sims
Published in *The Lifeboat*, August 1882)

10

Rick Rescorla 1939–2001

The Cornish Hero of the Twin Towers

'True heroes, by the nature of things, come along but rarely – and when they do we should be grateful that humankind, which is capable of so much that is abhorrent and evil, now and then produces an exceptional human being.'

(David Prowse: *Western Morning News*, 11.02.03)

Tuesday, 11th September 2001 was a day which changed the world forever. When the first aeroplane struck the tower of the prestigious World Trade Center in New York on that fateful day, many took it to be a tragic aviation accident, while those who happened to turn on their TV sets as a second plane came on the scene and crashed into the remaining tower thought they had tuned into a spectacular film drama. The unfolding news of the worst terrorist strike in history sent shock waves across the globe.

'Horror and disbelief is how America has reacted to Tuesday's tragedy,' reported former Penwith journalist Richard Mineards, who had been living in Manhattan for the last 25 years, and had just moved to California. Strangely, he had been alerted to the catastrophic situation by a concerned friend in Cornwall. He said that it was almost surreal as the shell-shocked Americans began to realise the full-scale of the disaster. One of his friends living nearby had gone up to his roof garden after the first crash, and actually saw the explosion as the second plane struck. He said it was unbelievable, like something out of *Towering Inferno* (filmed in 1974), only this was for real.

The tragic events in America, where so many Cornish miners

had emigrated when times were hard, touched the hearts of people across Cornwall; as in many counties and countries, special church services took place and books of remembrance were signed. It was quite a challenge for preachers to make any sense of such a negative situation and come up with a suitable message of hope. The congregation at St Petroc's church in the old garrison town of Bodmin, where the altar was draped with an American flag, heard Captain Walter Scull, the senior American officer at RAF St Mawgan, read a simple, fitting extract from the Book of Isaiah: 'He has sent me to bind up the broken hearted'. Father Graham Minors had opened the service with familiar words of comfort: 'I am the resurrection and the life, says the Lord. Those who believe in me will never die.' In his sermon he spoke of the difficulty of knowing what to say after a tragedy on this scale, and said that people often asked him what he felt about forgiveness. He believed in forgiveness but also in justice without vengeance. 'Forgiveness does have a price. There has to be repentance in order to forgive.' Bodmin man Simon Munn may have been thinking, 'There but for the grace of God go I,' for he would probably have been working in the World Trade Center, which was struck by the first aircraft, had he not been recently promoted.

Cornwall's Chief Fire Officer paid tribute to his counterpart in New York, who lost his life along with many of his men as they tried to rescue survivors, and the firemen of St Austell set up a fund to help the grieving families. Cornwall's Chief Fire Safety Officer said that they had been overwhelmed by the generosity of the people of Cornwall.

As more details of the atrocity began to filter out over the next few days, there were press reports that a Vietnam War veteran, born and brought up in Cornwall, was missing, feared dead, after heroically saving the lives of nearly 3,000 people caught up in the terrorist attacks on the World Trade Center. On 17th September, the *Western Morning News* carried the headline

'Disaster Hero Who Saved Thousands', while *The Cornishman*, which covers the Penwith area, sounded a more personal note, sadly proclaiming: 'Hayle's New York Hero Feared Dead'. When this tragic news was confirmed, a memorial service was held to honour the larger-than-life hero Rick Rescorla in his home town of Hayle.

Cyril Richard Rescorla was born in Hayle in 1939. He was a bright, talkative child with an inquiring mind and great zest for life, who enjoyed singing and reading books from a very early age. He loved the harbour and the great outdoors with the freedom to create his own adventures around the stimulating environment of Hayle. As he grew older he enjoyed his visits to the cinema, where the films he saw opened up a new and exciting world far beyond these much loved Cornish horizons, and he related to the American way of life. Hero worshipping the US

The harbourside at Hayle where Rick grew up. (Sheila Bird)

boxer Tami Moriello, who came over here and knocked out the British heavyweight champion in the 1940s, earned him the childhood nickname of 'Tami' amongst his local friends. He attended Penzance County Grammar School, travelling daily on the railway which skirts Mount's Bay. He excelled at rugby, and could have become a professional player. However, the seeds of adventure had already been sown, and the firm foundation of caring family, friends and traditional Cornish values stood him in good stead as an Action Man of the future. He also retained his passion for books and writing and was influenced by the works of writers such as Kipling, In fact his unfolding life story is reminiscent of manly, courageous characters in adventure stories, and an associate was later to reflect that much of his life was building up to that final, heroic moment of glory.

Rick left Hayle at the age of 18 and headed for London, to train with the Metropolitan Police. He then went overseas, serving as a police officer in former Rhodesia before going on to Cyprus and eventually arriving in America at the age of 23. He joined the US Army, got sent to Vietnam and became a legend there on account of his heroic actions. However, this was no gung-ho hero wallowing in the limelight, but a modest chap and natural leader who did what he thought was right.

Rescorla was a young lieutenant in the 2nd Battalion of the 7th Air Cavalry and displayed outstanding qualities in one of the bloodiest and most significant battles of the Vietnam War. He won the respect of US army colleagues and was regarded as one of the bravest soldiers they had ever seen. He was an inspiration on the battlefield and older brother figure off it. Sam Fantino, who met Rick in 1965, and became his radio operator in Vietnam, recalled, 'Rick had the unusual ability to not only lead his men but to be able to give us the confidence, the courage and the ability to do things that you never thought you could do in the face of such horrors.' He cited the battle fought in Ia Drang Valley after the Battalion's C Company had been overrun by the enemy and suffered heavy losses. Rick instructed his men to dig their foxholes and clear their field of fire. 'Despite the danger he walked about the foxholes like he was taking a stroll, whistling and singing while everybody else was cowering in the bottom of their holes. For us it was like, if he can do that, then we can do this. It was like that time after time in Vietnam.'

Bud Alley, another lieutenant in the 7th Cavalry, reflected, 'He was a man's man. He was just so full of life and absolutely fearless in battle. He was the bravest man I have ever known, and the most generous. From General Hal Moore at the top to the privates at the bottom, they would tell you that he was fearless and a leader of men.'

Rick applied for American citizenship after serving in Vietnam, to enable him to go to college on a GI scholarship and move up the ranks. He had become a colonel in the Army Reserve when he retired from service life in 1989. The lad from Hayle was to prove himself as an academic as well as a man-of-action, for having put himself through college at the University of Oklahoma, he went on to gain a master's degree in English and a degree in law, and demonstrated a flair for teaching.

During all his years spent overseas, Rick made frequent visits to see his family back in Cornwall, look up old friends and revel in the much loved haunts of his childhood. There was nothing he liked better than an exhilarating walk on Trencrom Hill, where he hoped his ashes might one day be scattered.

Having honed his skills in various directions after leaving the army, Rick became an expert in the field of banking and financial security. He decided to pin his colours to the mast of the Morgan Stanley Dean Witter bank, housed in the World Trade Center in New York, where he became a vice president and head of security. When terrorists first stuck the Twin Towers in 1993, using a van packed with explosives, Rick leapt into action and was the very last person to leave the building, having kept others calm with singing and reassuring utterances, as in his army days. His old comrade Joe Galloway said, 'He stayed until he had gotten everyone out, and that is the nature of the man!' In fact Rick had predicted just such a happening three years previously, with an eerie degree of accuracy. However, this and various other warnings, including possible attacks by air were ignored by the politicians.

A BBC documentary filmed in 1998, but not screened until February 2001, demonstrated the charismatic nature of Rick Rescorla. It transpired that Rick and Dan Hill, who first met Rick in 1965 at Officer Candidate School, used to discuss how an attack was likely to happen. Dan Hill said, 'He and I together figured the way it would happen. We thought it would be a cargo aircraft coming from the Middle East or from Europe. It would be loaded up with demolition and it would fly into one of the buildings about two thirds of the way up. If they penetrated deep enough the heat of the blast would cause the structured integrity to disintegrate and topple and a third of the building would collapse, and the overload would take the rest of the building down with it.' This is exactly what happened.

During that 1998 interview it became apparent that Rick had warned the American politicians to take heed of the 1993 attack. He commented that they were a de facto head of the United Nations, and first and foremost in the front line for a terrorist attack. Troops were fighting wars that the American people did not understand in places that they had never heard of, with names that they could not pronounce. He pointed out, 'We can't even straighten up our own capital in terms of crime, and we think we can go out there and be the world's top cop! It's impossible.' He said that things would come home to roost, with soldiers without uniforms waging wars on the streets of major cities. He warned, 'In the future we are going to see some action we've never seen before. They choose their time and their place. They hit and then they disperse.'

Rick's life took another turn in 1998. He was diagnosed with prostate cancer, and, although given only six months to live, was able to beat the disease after following a holistic approach to treatment. Then he met a bright and lively American woman, and she turned out to be his soulmate. The woman destined to be Rick's wife had been living in the same town house complex, and, while out walking her dog, had stopped to ask him why he was jogging in bare feet. He explained that he was writing a book about Rhodesia and wanted to experience how it felt to run with no shoes on, and an immediate rapport was established. They had a quiet wedding in Florida, and Rick brought his new bride home to Hayle to meet his family and friends and introduced her to the haunts of his childhood. On their second trip to Hayle in 1999 Rick took her along to the ancient church in Lelant, where his grandparents were buried, and they renewed their wedding vows on a bench beneath one of the beautiful trees in the churchyard.

Early on the morning of 11th September 2001, Rick set off for work as usual, and his wife Susan called him at 8.15 to tell him she loved him. When she heard of the air attack on the World Trade Center she called his office and was told, 'Don't worry about anything. Rick is getting people out.' She was anxious and tearful and the last communication she had with her husband was when he called her on his cell phone. He told her not to cry. He was helping everyone evacuate, but if something happened to him, he wanted her to know she had 'made his life'. Dan Hill got a phone call from Rick to alert him to the possibility that this could be the terrorist attack they had predicted. Dan agreed that it could be a hit and asked him what he was doing. 'I'm getting my people the hell out of here . . . Those idiots from Port Authority are telling them to stay at their stations . . . '

Rick went from floor to floor making sure that people were out, and calmly directing operations through a megaphone. Bob Sloss, a managing director at Morgan Stanley, who last saw Rick on the 10th floor in the stairwell said, 'He was definitely there well after it had been established that the building was in trouble. I was told by the chief executive of Morgan Stanley that Rick was observed by many as cool and calm, leading people out, saying "God Bless America", "Peace to you" and singing to them to ease the panic.' He always included some Cornish songs learnt in childhood.

Rick had plenty of opportunity to escape from the southern tower, but that was not the nature of the man. With no thought for himself, he made his way up the building seeking out anyone who might be trapped, injured or confused. As the devastating consequences of the terrorist attacks carried out by suicide squads began to emerge before an outraged world audience, the man from Hayle was still saving others. 'He couldn't be any other way,' remarked Sam Fantino.

The memorial to Rick Rescorla on the harbourside at Hayle bears an inscription which begins: Cyril Richard 'Rick' Rescorla. Hayle 1939–2001 New York. (Sheila Bird)

The last photograph of him on the 42nd floor with megaphone in hand, taken by his secretary, was beamed across the world. It captured a hero at his professional best, calmly helping others to safety. Minutes later the giant building collapsed and he was never seen again. His heartbroken widow declared, 'My Rick has spread his wings and soared into Eternity.'

In July 2002, Rick Rescorla was given a posthumous British Gold Hero Award. On the first anniversary of the atrocity, Susan Rescorla wore a vermilion blazer (in deference to Rick's aversion to mournful colours) as she went to a Ground Zero special morning of commemoration in New York, and she and her family later attended a memorial service to British victims of the attack at St Thomas church in New York, which was also attended by over 300 British police and firemen. In Britain an open air memorial service was held at RAF St Mawgan, to pay tribute to their fellow Americans who died during the terrorist attacks, and people went to the church services across the West Country. In Hayle a granite memorial to the local hero was unveiled by his cousin Jon Daniels, landlord of the Cornish Arms. In October 2003 Susan, who had a great empathy with Hayle and its people, was presented with a special bravery award set in Cornish tin from the Cornish Stannary Parliament. She also visited the Rick Rescorla wildlife garden at Penpol Primary School, where her husband had been a pupil. In his presentation speech Stannator Dr Nigel Hicks declared, 'Rick Rescorla has now joined the ranks of the Cornish greats . . .'

Bibliography

Allen, John, *The History of Liskeard*, 1855
Baring Gould, S., *Cornish Characters and Strange Events*, 1909
Baring Gould, S., *The Vicar of Morwenstow*
Barnes, Peter, *Alfred Wallis and His Family Fact and Fiction*
Berlin, Sven, *Alfred Wallis Primitive*, 1942
Bird, Sheila, *Cornish Curiosities*, 1989
Bird, Sheila, *Mayday! Preserving Life from Shipwreck off Cornwall*, 1991
Bray, Billy, *The King's Son*
Brendon, Piers, *Hawker of Morwenstow, 1975*
Byles, C.E., *The Life and Letters of R.S. Hawker*
Carew, Richard, *Survey of Cornwall*, 1602
Cook, Judith, *To Brave Every Danger*, 1993
Corin, John, Farr, Grahame, *Penlee Lifeboat*, 1983
Currey, C.H., *The Transportation, Escape and Pardoning of Mary Bryant*
Daniell, Rev J.J., Thurston, Peter C., *History and Geography of Cornwall*, 1893
Davey, Cyril, *The Glory Man*
Davey, F. Hamilton, *Neville Northey Burnard*, 1909
Greenhill, Basil, *Merchant Schooners*
Halliday, F.E., *A History of Cornwall*, 1959
Harris, J. Henry, *Cornish Saints and Sinners*, 1906
Harris, Wilson, *Caroline Fox*, 1944
Hodge, James, *Richard Trevithick*
Lee, Rev Frederick George, *Memorials of the Late Rev Stephen Hawker, MA*
Martin, Mary, *A Wayward Genius Neville Northey Burnard*, 1978
Rolt, L.T.C., *The Cornish Giant*, 1960
Sagar Fenton, Michael, *The Loss of a Lifeboat*, 1991

BIBILIOGRAPHY

Stewart, James B., *Heart of a Soldier*
Trevithick, Francis, *Life of Richard Trevithick*
Lake's Parochial *History of Cornwall*

The Cornishman, West Briton, Cornish Guardian, Daily Telegraph, Sherborne Mercury, Western Morning News
Old Cornwall Vol 11, Parts 1 12, 1991, 1997: Dolly Pentreath: Dr R.J. Pentreath
Vol 12, 1 2, 1997, 2003: More About Dolly Pentreath: Michael Tangye
Cornwall Today Vol 1, No 1, 1994
Vol 1, No 2, 1994
Horizon Vol VII, No 37, 1943
Cornish Scene, 8, 14, 1990, 1992

Index

INDEX